An Informative Guide for Leisurely Motoring or

BICYCLING
SAN LUIS OBISPO COUNTY

by Sharon Lewis Dickerson

Photography by Joseph A. Dickerson

Illustrations by Marti Fast

EZ Nature Books
San Luis Obispo, California

*for Joe — may we always ride in tandem
and
for Mom and Dad — for believing in their
"black sheep"*

ACKNOWLEDGEMENTS

Ralph and Laverne Boethling of the Great Western Bicycle Rally for their input on North County rides; **Margot Comstock** for her patient and effective Macintosh training; **Jim Delany** for his input on routes and his critique of the manuscript; **Marti Fast** for her artistic input, support and friendship; **Warren Hansen** for his input on routes and support; **Ira Hughes** for his continued willingness to help with my cycling projects; **Stu and Janie Goldenberg** for their input on favorite rides; and **Ed Zolkoski** for the opportunity.

CONTENTS

INTRODUCTION

If you're fond of sand dunes and salty air ... not to mention sleepy rural towns, flower-filled meadows, red-tiled missions, oak-dotted hills and quiet country roads ... you're sure to fall in love with San Luis Obispo County over the handlebars.

Located halfway between San Francisco and Los Angeles on California's beautiful central coast, San Luis Obispo County is divided naturally into three sections — South County and the city of San Luis Obispo, North Coast and North County. Each area has its own character based on terrain, history and microclimate. And, each offers spectacular cycling possibilities.

Cycling in San Luis Obispo County is a year-round activity. Temperatures average about 60 to 70 degrees along the coast, but in the northern inland areas it is not unusual for the mercury to plummet to 20 degrees on a cold winter morning or soar to 100 plus degrees on a hot summer day. Fog is always a possibility along the coast, but it is most prevalent during spring and summer. No matter what the season, it's best to layer clothing and carry a jacket.

The prevailing wind in the county is from the west and the north. Along the coast it blows from north to south. However, it can swirl through the canyons and valleys somewhat unpredictably. When possible, I've tried to route the rides to make use of the prevailing wind. Since it usually comes up in the afternoon, you can reduce your chances of having to battle strong gusts by riding in the morning. Wind is a factor yearround, but predominantly in the summer.

I've rated the rides according to my personal bias which, I think, is fairly average for an active cyclist. If you can ride 50 miles in four to five hours without much difficulty, the ratings should hold fairly true. If you're not comfortable doing that much — or can easily do more — you'll have to adjust the ratings accordingly. And, of course, remember the ease or difficulty of a ride can vary from day to day depending on weather, traffic and your general state of mind. All things considered, *easy* means flat or rolling; *moderate* means flat or rolling with some climbs; *difficult* means there is at least one major climb that makes me wonder why I consider cycling "fun"; and, *very difficult* means exactly that — long and hard, but rewarding in terms of scenery and accomplishment.

Enjoy your travels. And, may the dogs you encounter be friendly, the flats be few and far between and the wind be always at your back.

4

San Luis Obispo County

San Miguel

San Simeon
Paso Robles

Cambria
Templeton
Atascadero

Pacific
Cayucos
Morro Bay
Santa Margarita

Ocean
San Luis Obispo

Avila Beach
Pismo Beach
Oceano
Arroyo Grande
Nipomo

Pacific Ocean

Bicycle Rentals of Pismo Beach, 930 Price Street, Pismo Beach, 773-2215.

Broad Street Bikes, 741 Humbert Avenue (between South and Orcutt), San Luis Obispo, 541-5878.

Grand Schwinn Shop, 983 Grand Avenue, Grover City, 481-3292.

Ira's Bike Shop, 107 Bridge Street, Arroyo Grande, 489-2621.

Ken's Bicycle Shop, 1235 Monterey Street, San Luis Obispo, 543-8179.

Pete's Bicycle Shop, 1124 Garden Street, San Luis Obispo, 543-7045.

Pro Spoke Cyclery, 971 Higuera Street, San Luis Obispo, 541-3600.

Spirit Cycle Works, 399 Foothill Boulevard, San Luis Obispo, 541-5673.

Velo SLO, 198 South Street, San Luis Obispo, 543-4416.

5

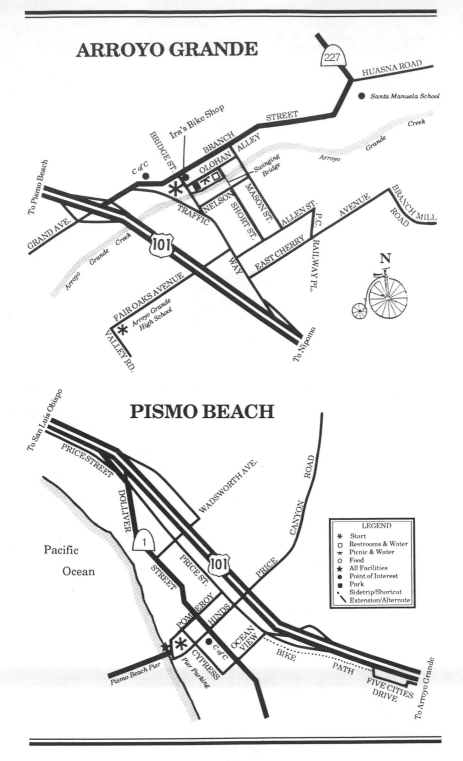

ARROYO GRANDE

227

HUASNA ROAD

● Santa Manuela School

Ira's Bike Shop

STREET

BRIDGE ST.

BRANCH

OLOHAN

ALLEY

C of C

Swinging Bridge

Creek

Grande

Arroyo

NELSON

MASON ST.

SHORT ST.

ALLEN ST.

P.C. RAILWAY PL.

AVENUE

BRANCH MILL ROAD

TRAFFIC

GRAND AVE.

To Pismo Beach

Arroyo Grande Creek

101

WAY

EAST CHERRY

N

FAIR OAKS AVENUE

Arroyo Grande High School

VALLEY RD.

To Nipomo

PISMO BEACH

To San Luis Obispo

PRICE STREET

DOLLIVER

WADSWORTH AVE.

CANYON ROAD

Pacific Ocean

1

PRICE ST.

101

PRICE

STREET

POMEROY

HINDS

OCEAN VIEW

C of C

●

CYPRESS

Pismo Beach Pier

Pier Parking

BIKE

PATH

FIVE CITIES DRIVE

To Arroyo Grande

LEGEND	
✳	Start
□	Restrooms & Water
☂	Picnic & Water
○	Food
★	All Facilities
●	Point of Interest
■	Park
⋰	Sidetrip/Shortcut
⟍	Extension/Alternate

SAN LUIS OBISPO

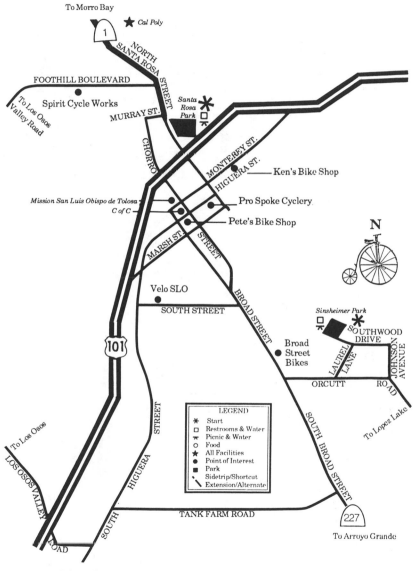

To Morro Bay

★ Cal Poly

1

NORTH SANTA ROSA STREET

FOOTHILL BOULEVARD

To Los Osos Valley Road

● Spirit Cycle Works

MURRAY ST.

Santa Rosa Park ✳ ▫ ⊼

CHORRO

MONTEREY ST.

HIGUERA ST.

● Ken's Bike Shop

Mission San Luis Obispo de Tolosa
C of C ●

● ● Pro Spoke Cyclery

● Pete's Bike Shop

MARSH ST.

STREET

N

● Velo SLO

SOUTH STREET

BROAD STREET

Sinsheimer Park

▫ ⊼ ✳ SOUTHWOOD DRIVE

Broad Street Bikes ●

LAUREL LANE

JOHNSON AVENUE

ORCUTT   ROAD

To Lopez Lake

SOUTH BROAD STREET

HIGUERA STREET

To Los Osos

LOS OSOS VALLEY

LEGEND
✳ Start
▫ Restrooms & Water
⊼ Picnic & Water
○ Food
★ All Facilities
● Point of Interest
■ Park
⟍ Sidetrip/Shortcut
⟍ Extension/Alternate

TANK FARM ROAD

SOUTH ROAD

227

To Arroyo Grande

To Avila Beach/Pismo Beach

101

Arroyo Grande

Arroyo Grande
High School

FAIR OAKS AVE.

VALLEY RD.

Sunrise Center
Rose Victorian Inn

LOS

Hamilton Nursery

1

BERROS

Young's Nursery

Chase's Olives

101

Los Berros Store
Los Berros School

ROAD

Oso Flaco Lake

LEGEND
✳ Start
☐ Restrooms & Water
☂ Picnic & Water
○ Food
★ All Facilities
● Point of Interest
■ Park
⟍ Sidetrip/Shortcut
⟍ Extension/Alternate

Black Lake Golf Course

WILLOW ROAD

N. THOMPSON AVE.

Summit Station

OSO

FLACO

1

Kaminaka
U-Pick-Em Farms

POMEROY RD.

MELSCHAU RD.

DANA FOOTHILL RD.

LAKE

Jocko's

Nipomo Regional Park

Church

ROAD

WEST
TEFFT

E. TEFFT ST.

OAKGLEN AVE.

Scale of Miles

DIVISION

STREET

ORCHARD

Dana Adobe

0   1   2   3   4

Nipomo

1 — NIPOMO AND OSO FLACO LAKE
RIDE AT A GLANCE

DISTANCE:	37 miles
TRAFFIC:	light to moderate
BIKE LANE:	good shoulder in heavier traffic areas
RATING:	difficult
SHORTCUT:	moderate 26 miles, skips Oso Flaco Lake
CAUTION:	Traffic on Highway 1 on the Nipomo Mesa can be erratic on summer afternoons and weekends. Speedsters and lookiloos are the problem. Ride early in the day, if possible.

A Victorian home painted several shades of rose. An 1890s schoolhouse. A mountain shaped like a clam. An adobe that once was the site of lavish fiestas. A freshwater lake nestled in sand dunes that roll to the sea. The pungent aroma of eucalyptus. These are just a few of the special treats you encounter on this ride through the southernmost reaches of San Luis Obispo County.

You pedal through the gently rolling hills of Arroyo Grande and Los Berros and the flat produce fields of the Nipomo and Guadalupe valleys before climbing up — and sliding down! — the Nipomo Mesa. It's a challenge at times, but definitely worth the effort.

Start the ride at Arroyo Grande High School (0.0) on the corner of Fair Oaks Avenue and Valley Road (see the Arroyo Grande map at the beginning of this section). In the summer and on weekends, you can use the high school parking lot. When school is in session, there is limited on-street parking.

Head south along Valley Road. Sunrise Shopping Center (.7) has a good market. It's your last guaranteed chance for food or water before Nipomo. Right next to the Center is the Rose Victorian Inn. This 14 room home — referred to by local historians as the Pitkin-Conrow house or the Parker-Davis house — was built around 1885 by Charles Allan Pitkin who farmed 53 acres and introduced English walnuts to the area. His trees flourished and it's said that the finest walnuts in the world were grown in the Arroyo Grande valley with crops peaking in the 1920s and 1930s. But urbanization took its toll, and today only a few walnut groves remain. Today the landmark home is a bed and breakfast inn with beautiful gardens and a cozy restaurant that's open to the public.

9

Rose Victorian Inn, Arroyo Grande.

Turn left on Los Berros Road (.9). Sycamore and oak-covered hills hug the right side of this narrow, winding country road; produce fields framed by gentle hills — golden in the summer and fall, velvety green in winter and spring — spread out to the left. The road climbs very gently until at 3.3 miles you come to the Los Berros Store and the small community of Los Berros.

"Berro" is Spanish for "watercress" and it is believed the Spaniards in the Portolá expedition of 1769 named the area for the watercress they gathered in streams and lakes along their way. More than a century later, Los Berros was a flourishing agricultural area and the school built in 1891 to educate local children stands today, nestled against the bluffs of the Nipomo Mesa on your right. It's a private residence now, but you can get a good look at the outside of the building by taking any of the sidestreets off Los Berros Road.

At 5.6 miles, Los Berros Road crosses under Highway 101 and becomes North Thompson Avenue. Just past the underpass, look for Old Summit Road (6.1) on the right. Not far up the road, a house marks Summit Station, the highest point on the Pacific Coast Railway — a narrow gauge system that ran from Avila Beach to Los Olivos from the late 1800s to the early 1940s. And, it was on this knoll that Captain John Frémont and 430 of his soldiers camped in 1846 on their way to Los Angeles.

Continue on North Thompson, a lightly traveled road that roller-coasters through horse ranches, farms and citrus and avocado groves. Turn left on Mehlschau Road (7.9). Directly ahead is Clamshell Mountain. Mehlschau Road ends at Dana Foothill Road (8.9). Turn right and follow the line of the Nipomo foothills to East Tefft (10.0) and turn right again. East Tefft — named for Henry Tefft, the county's first assemblyman — leads into the town of Nipomo.

Nipomo is the name given to the 37,888 acre rancho granted to William Goodwin Dana in 1837. That name is a variation on the Chumash, "Nepomah", meaning "at the foot of the hills".

Thompson Avenue (11.3) is the main drag in Nipomo. The old St. Joseph's Catholic Church — on the northeast corner of this intersection — was built in 1902. Since the new church was built in 1970, this building has housed a number of commercial businesses — one a professional stained glass craftsman who restored the beautiful windows. Directly across the street is Jocko's, a popular steakhouse and wateringhole. Just one block to the south, on the southeast corner of Thompson Avenue and Dana Street, is a beautiful Victorian home. Built by U.S. Runels in 1887, the house was purchased several years later by Joseph Dana, one of the original pioneers of the area, and used as a boarding home. The house remained in the Dana family until the early 1960s. Today it's the Kaleidoscope Inn, a bed and breakfast establishment. (Mileage to the inn is not included in the total miles.)

Stay on East Tefft and cross Thompson Avenue. You're now on West Tefft. Food and water are available at the Adobe Plaza (11.6). Turn left on Oakglen Avenue (11.8) and follow this road to the Dana Adobe (12.8). Dana, a retired sea captain and one time alcalde (mayor) of Santa Barbara (his cousin, Richard Henry Dana wrote Two Years Before the Mast) built this home in 1839 to accommodate his 13 children. It became *the* stopping place for people traveling between Santa Barbara and San Luis Obispo. Many dignitaries were entertained here and lavish, multi-day fiestas which included food and wine, music, dance, bullfights, cockfights and horse races were common. Today the adobe is owned by the San Luis Obispo County Historical Society and is open to the public only on special occasions.

Return to West Tefft (13.9) and turn left. At 14.0 miles, Tefft crosses over Highway 101. There's a gas station on the east side of the freeway if you're in need of water or a restroom. And, there's a market and restaurant (14.2) on the west side. Stay on Tefft as it roller-coasters through a mix of mini-ranches and new homes. It's 4-H country. Here a horse, there a cow, everywhere a sheep or a pig.

11

If you're going to take the SHORTCUT, turn right on Pomeroy Road (14.6) and follow the SHORTCUT directions. Nipomo Regional Park is at this intersection. Restrooms, picnic and barbecue facilities, hiking trails, baseball diamonds, a children's playground and water are available. *If you're going to Oso Flaco Lake, stay on West Tefft and turn left on Orchard Road (14.9), then right on Division Street (15.6).* There's a market on the southeast corner. If you need food or water, get it now because you won't get another chance for 17 miles.

At 16.6 miles, you begin a fast descent off the Nipomo Mesa. Be careful. The road is narrow and there are some sharp turns. But, the view and the ride are wonderful. Once off the mesa, you're in the heart of the South County's agricultural land. The road is flat and narrow, with no shoulder, and passes right through the fields. During harvesting, you often have to dodge dirt clods and tractors. But there's not much traffic, and what there is moves very slowly.

Turn right on Oso Flaco Lake Road (18.9), then cross Highway 1 (21.1) and continue through the fields of broccoli, cabbage, Brussels sprouts and what have you to Oso Flaco Lake (24.3). There's a parking lot here, but you can ride your bike on the wide, paved trail that leads to the lake. (The trail is about 1/2 mile long. This mileage is not included in the mileage totals.)

Oso Flaco (Skinny Bear) Lake was named by the Don Gaspar de Portolá expedition that camped here in September, 1769. Tired and hungry, the men shot a grizzly bear — a skinny one evidently — and had him for dinner. They supplemented their bear meat with watercress, wild gooseberries and strawberries. Not much has changed since the Spaniards marched through. The round lake still sparkles in the sunlight surrounded by dunes and cattails. There are ducks, teals, red-winged black birds, cormorants, dragonflies and many shore birds. Only the grizzlies are gone. Be sure to take your binoculars and camera and food for a picnic.

After enjoying the lake, backtrack to Highway 1 (27.5) and turn left. Up ahead is the Nipomo Mesa. The climb, which starts at 28.0 miles and crests at 29.1 miles isn't as bad as it looks from this vantage point. In between the pulls are some rollies, but the general direction is up.

Eucalyptus are very prominent on the mesa. Thousands of the trees were planted as seedlings in 1908 by two men who formed the Los Berros Forest Company. The idea was to sell the trees as hardwood. But, when the eucalyptus didn't yield good building timber, the project was abandoned. The forest, though, is still here and provides shade and wonderful aromas.

At Willow Road (30.3), Highway 1 makes a sharp turn to the left. *If you opted for the SHORTCUT, this is where you rejoin the main route. The second number in the parentheses represents your mileage.* The road continues to roller-coaster through sagebrush and eucalyptus, past the Union Oil Refinery and a smattering of homes. Chase's Olives (33.0/22.1), a family-operated roadside stand, sells a variety of olives which they cure themselves, along with nuts, honey, dates, soft drinks and a few arts and crafts. There is no public restroom, but there is water and a small picnic area.

Highway 1 continues its up and down undulations past Young's Mesa Geranium Nursery (33.3/22.4), a gas station and market (34.3/23.4) and Hamilton Orchid Nursery (34.5/23.6) before plunging down to the Arroyo Grande lowlands. The view is breathtaking, but the descent is fast, steep and winding and it's likely you'll only see the pavement in front of you. At 35.6/24.7 miles turn right on Valley Road and head for the high school (36.9/26.0).

If you've got the strength, pedal over to the flagpole at the front of the school. Forming the base is a huge millstone. Brought by ship from Mexico in 1844, the historic stone was used at the Branch grist mill, located east of the Village of Arroyo Grande. The mill is gone, but the stone remains as a reminder of Arroyo Grande's rich heritage.

SHORTCUT

Follow West Tefft Street to Pomeroy Road (14.6) and turn right. The Nipomo Regional Park on your left has water, rest-rooms, picnic and barbecue facilities, hiking trails, baseball diamonds, a children's playground and more.

Pomeroy Road is narrow and winding at this point. You pedal through oaks and eucalyptus, mini-ranches, farm stands selling fresh produce and a varied assortment of homes. Kaminaka U-Pick-Em Farms (16.2) is just what it says. You can pick your own fresh fruits, berries and veggies in season. Check the sign at the entrance for seasonal hours.

Turn left on Willow Road (16.9) following the signs to Black Lake Golf Course. The road is pleasantly wide with a marked shoulder. Entrance to the golf course is at Black Lake Canyon Drive (17.5). If you're in need of food, water or restrooms, they're available at the golf course which is open to the public. After the golf course (18.4), the road narrows and roller-coasters through eucalyptus, vineyards and citrus groves until it intersects with Highway 1 (19.4). *Rejoin the main route at this point.*

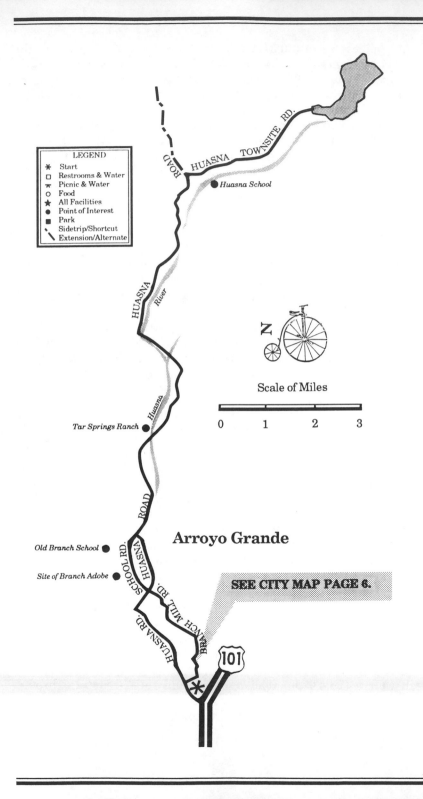

LEGEND
* Start
□ Restrooms & Water
⊼ Picnic & Water
○ Food
★ All Facilities
● Point of Interest
■ Park
. Sidetrip/Shortcut
\ Extension/Alternate

HUASNA TOWNSITE RD.

ROAD

● Huasna School

HUASNA

River

N

Scale of Miles

0   1   2   3

Huasna

Tar Springs Ranch ●

ROAD

Arroyo Grande

Old Branch School ●

Site of Branch Adobe ●

SCHOOL RD.

HUASNA

SEE CITY MAP PAGE 6.

HUASNA RD.

BRANCH MILL RD.

101

*

2 — THE HUASNA VALLEY

RIDE AT A GLANCE

DISTANCE: 32 miles
TRAFFIC: light to moderate
BIKE LANE: good shoulder in higher traffic areas
RATING: moderate to difficult
SIDETRIP: very difficult 5.2 mile loop to Huasna
                 River
CAUTION: no food, water or restrooms in the valley

W-A-U-Z-N-A. That spelling wouldn't win any bees, but it's closer to "Wasna", the ancient Chumash Indian spelling, than H-U-A-S-N-A, today's version. No matter how you spell it, tho Huacna Valloy and tho road that loado to it io a dclight. According to Chumash legend, the Huasna Valley is the stairway to the heavens. Once you've visited this area, you'll see why. Except for the farms and ranches that dot the landscape, the area hasn't changed much since 1843 when Isaac J. Sparks was granted 22,153 acres dubbed Rancho Huasna. It's open and wild — a throwback to simpler times.

Start the ride in the parking lot (called Olohan Alley) behind **Ira's Bike Shop** in the Village of Arroyo Grande (see the Arroyo Grande map at the beginning of this section). Walk up to the gazebo and across the Swinging Bridge. This 171 foot suspension footbridge that spans Arroyo Grande Creek was originally built by Newton Short in the 1880s to connect his home on one side of the creek with his orchard on the other. It was washed out by floods several times during ensuing years, but always rebuilt. In 1911, the Short family gave it to the City of Arroyo Grande. The bridge was completely renovated in 1969 and it is recognized as an official San Luis Obispo County Historical Landmark.

Once across the bridge, you're in the residential section of the Village. Mount your steed, start your odometer (0.0) and pedal past Victorians and bungalows — the two-story home at 213 was Newton Short's — to Allen Street (.2). Turn left, then right on P.C. Railway Place (.4). This little bit of road is named for the Pacific Coast Railway that ran from Port Harford (Avila Beach) to San Luis Obispo and Edna in the north, then through Arroyo Grande to Nipomo, Santa Maria, Orcutt, Los Alamos and Los Olivos in the south. The narrow gauge railroad carried passengers and freight from 1876 to 1942 and served as a major influence in the development of agriculture and commerce.

15

P.C. Railway Place ends at East Cherry Avenue (.5). Turn left. The road makes a tight turn to the right (.7) and becomes Branch Mill Road. In the blink of an eye, you're out of town, pedaling along a country road bordered by lush produce fields on the left and densely forested oak-covered hills on the right. Branch Mill Road is narrow, winding and very "country". Watch out for dirt clods and other debris on the road during harvest times. The road, though, is lightly traveled and a pure joy to ride. Keep your eyes peeled for "garden goodies" signs. Several people in the area put seasonal produce out in small stands along the road. It's the honor system. You just take what you want and drop the money in a jar.

The Branch Mill area got its name from a grist and flour mill operated by Ramon Branch — son of Francis Z. Branch, original grantee of the Santa Manuela Rancho. The mill operated from the early 1840s until the mid-1890s and used two large mill stones, made in Mexico of volcanic rock. Today, thanks to the Arroyo Grande Women's Club, one of those stones forms the base of the flagpole at Arroyo Grande High School.

Newsom Springs Road (1.4) was once the stagecoach road that ran over Newsom Ridge to Los Berros Road and Rancho Nipomo. Along the way was Newsom's White Sulphur Springs, a resort that catered to the area's prominent citizens who came to bathe in the warm sulphur waters. The resort, which operated from 1870 to 1890 is gone, but the springs remain. Unfortunately, the road leading to them is private.

Stay on Branch Mill Road until it meets Huasna Road (2.9) and turn right. At the stop sign (4.2), continue to follow Huasna Road by turning right again.

The Huasna Road is a roller coaster affair, winding and climbing through vast expanses of farmland, open range land and rolling hills — golden in summer and early fall, velvety green in winter, and ablaze with the blues and yellows of wild-flowers in spring.

At 9.6 miles you pass Tar Springs Ranch. An area land-mark, the ranch is named for the asphaltum that covers the land in big beds and soft pools. This substance was found in great quantities on the Huasna and Santa Manuela Ranchos and was used by the rancheros to waterproof roofs and lubricate the wheels of their wagons and buggies. Francis Z. Branch gave this portion of his holdings to his son, Frank, who developed the tar mines and shipped tar via the Pacific Coast Railway to Port Harford and then on to San Francisco.

After Tar Springs Ranch, the hills and trees begin to close in and you find yourself pedaling along a road shaded by a canopy of oaks and sycamores. About that same time, you notice you're

16

Windmills dot the Branch Mill and Huasna landscape.

beginning to climb (10.3). The climb starts in earnest at 10.8 miles and winds sharply. Then, just when you thought you didn't have anything left, you crest the hill (11.6) and fly into the Huasna Valley (12.1). Turn right on Huasna Townsite Road (12.9). The hand-lettered welcome sign, proclaiming Huasna's population at 171 and the elevation at 768, is courtesy of the Huasna Valley 4-H Club.

A little red schoolhouse, built in 1907, sits in a shaded glen on the right side of the road (13.0). It's no longer in use, but it did its part in educating many of the Huasna pioneers. Prior to the construction of this school, Huasna children learned their lessons under the shelter of a huge oak.

Continue on Huasna Townsite Road until you reach a wooden bridge which spans the Huasna River (15.9). At the far end of the bridge, the road turns to dirt and you turn around and head back the way you came. The setting is idyllic. Horses, cows, sheep and windmills dot the rolling landscape. Farm and ranch houses perch on top of grassy hills and snuggle in tree-lined valleys. All too soon, you're back at Huasna Road (19.0). *If you're going to take the SIDETRIP, turn right and follow the SIDETRIP directions. If not, turn left.*

To paraphrase a platitude, what goes down, must go up. And you, unfortunately, must climb back out of the valley. The steep climb begins at about 20.0/25.2 miles and continues for approximately 1/2 mile. Then, it's all downhill.

17

At the spot where Huasna Road turns off to the left (27.7/32.9), continue straight. You're now on School Road, named for the new Branch School (28.2/33.4). The original Branch School — a one-room schoolhouse — is now a private residence. To see it, turn right on Branch Mill Road (28.3). The rose-colored building is .4 miles down on your right. (This detour is not included in the total mileage.)

The site of the original Branch adobe (28.4/33.6) is just past Branch Mill Road on the right. The adobe crumbled years ago, but the site is marked by a large mound of earth, a gray shack and a willow tree. The cluster of palms and cypresses below it mark the site of a frame house built and occupied by Branch's son, Fred. The Branch flour mill was also located in this general vicinity.

Turn right on Huasna Road (29.2/34.4), then left on Huasna Road/Lopez Drive (29.7/34.9). At this point it will come as a rude shock to discover you're not in the boonies anymore. Traffic on Huasna Road/Lopez Drive can be heavy at times. But, there's a wide shoulder.

If you're in need of water or a restroom, Strother Park (30.5/35.7) makes a nice stop. If not, continue on to the junction of Huasna Road/Lopez Drive and Highway 227 (31.3/36.5) and turn left. The one-room schoolhouse on the corner once stood on the Santa Manuela Rancho in Lopez Canyon. Joseph N. Jatta, a pioneer rancher with 11 children in need of an education, donated the land for the school in 1877. The school was moved to its current location in 1986 by the South County Historical Society and is open to the public on weekends.

Follow Branch Street (Highway 227) to Mason Street (31.8/37.0), turn left, then right immediately into Olohan Alley. There are public restrooms near the gazebo and the town — founded in 1867 — offers a variety of eating, shopping and browsing experiences.

If you're too pooped to party, the Village Green and Kiwanis Park are great places to sit and reflect on the fact that you now share something in common with Alexi Grewal. Oh, did I forget to mention it? Alexi, the 1984 Olympic Gold Medalist, lived in San Luis Obispo County for a time during his high school years and the ride out to Huasna and back was one of his favorite training rides.

18

SIDETRIP

Return to Huasna Road (19.0) via Huasna Townsite Road and turn right. The road is rough and very narrow, winding through oaks dripping with moss. Watch for wildlife. I've seen a family of quail, a red-tailed hawk and a tarantula all within a quarter-mile stretch. There's a half-mile climb, beginning at 19.7 miles. It crests at a cattle guard (20.2) and you get a marvelous view of the Santa Lucia Range and the Los Padres National Forest. From there, you fly down steep, hairpin curves to the Huasna River (21.6) and a wood-planked bridge. Across the bridge, the road turns to dirt. That's where you turn around.

Now, the fun part. You get to go *up* what you came down. It's a challenge; one I don't recommend to the weak hearted. But, at 24.2 miles you're back at the junction of Huasna Road and Huasna Townsite Road. *Rejoin the main route at this point. The second number in the parentheses represents your total mileage.*

Site of the Branch adobe and flour mill, Branch Mill Road.

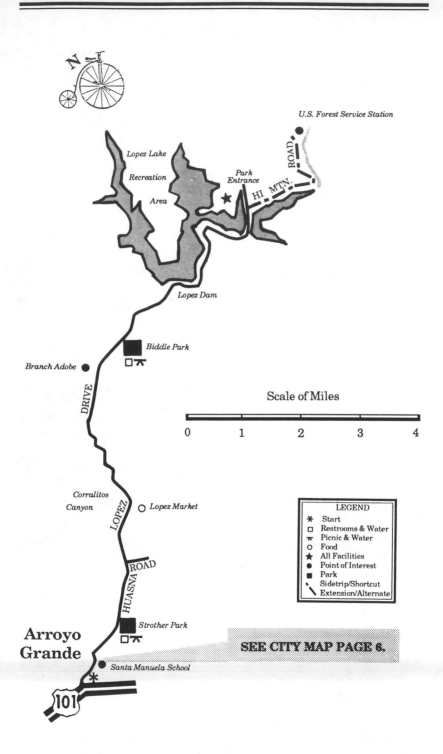

N

U.S. Forest Service Station

Lopez Lake

Recreation

Area

Park
Entrance

HI MTN. ROAD

Lopez Dam

Biddle Park

Branch Adobe

DRIVE

Scale of Miles

0   1   2   3   4

Corralitos
Canyon

LOPEZ

Lopez Market

ROAD

HUASNA

Strother Park

Arroyo
Grande

Santa Manuela School

101

LEGEND
* Start
□ Restrooms & Water
📯 Picnic & Water
○ Food
★ All Facilities
● Point of Interest
■ Park
🝿 Sidetrip/Shortcut
＼ Extension/Alternate

SEE CITY MAP PAGE 6.

3 — LOPEZ LAKE

RIDE AT A GLANCE

DISTANCE: 21 miles
TRAFFIC: light to heavy (summer and weekends)
BIKE LANE: good shoulder on Lopez Drive
RATING: easy to moderate
SIDETRIP: moderate 4.6 mile loop out Hi Mountain
                  Road to the Forest Service Station
CAUTION: Summer and weekend traffic can be
                  heavy —lots of motorhomes and cars
                  pulling boat trailers.

A lazy, sun-drenched picnic. A refreshing swim. A post-swim nap in the shade of a gnarled oak. A lakeside hike. These — if I may paraphrase Julie Andrews-cum-Maria Von Trapp — are a few of my fa-vor-ite things. Top them off with a leisurely pedal through oak-dotted hills and this ride, to me, is what two-wheeled travel is all about.

Lopez Lake, located just 11 miles east of the Village of Arroyo Grande, is, perhaps, the most popular lake in the county with 550,000 visitors annually. Fishing, swimming, sailing, picnicking and the always-popular Mustang Water Slide are the main attractions. There are 22 miles of shoreline, beautiful camping facilities, a marina, a general store and eight scenic hiking trails. Built by the Department of Parks and Beaches of San Luis Obispo County in 1969, the lake is part of the 4300-acre Lopez Recreation Area.

Start the ride in the parking lot (called Olohan Alley) behind **Ira's Bike Shop** in the Village of Arroyo Grande (see the Arroyo Grande map at the beginning of this section). Head east, along the Village Green and Arroyo Grande Creek, to the end of the alley (.1) and turn left on Mason Street. At the signal (.2) turn right on Branch Street. Continue on Branch (Highway 227), past a row of Victorian homes — a reminder of the Village's beginnings — to the intersection of Huasna Road (.6). At the stop, veer to the right, following the signs to Lopez Lake.

Once past the suburbs that have grown up around the Village, the landscape along Huasna (say Waz´na) Road turns to farm and ranch land dotted by the occasional house. Strother Park (1.3) marks the unofficial boundary between town and country. The park has picnic facilities, water and restrooms. At 2.2 miles, Huasna Road turns off to the right. Continue straight. The road is now called Lopez Drive.

21

Boating, swimming and relaxing are popular at Lopez Lake.

Lopez Drive climbs ever so gently along the arroyo dug by Arroyo Grande Creek. Oaks and sycamores crowd the creekbed and the side of the road, framed by the rolling foothills of the Santa Lucia Range. At 3.2 miles, Corralitos Canyon is off to the left. This area was farmed by the Spanish padres from Mission San Luis Obispo de Tolosa as early as 1780. According to diaries kept by the priests, large quantities of beans, potatoes, onions, chilies and other vegetables that would not grow well in the adobe soil along San Luis Creek were raised at the Corralitos asistencia. Across the street, Lopez Market (3.3) is your last chance for food or drink before the lake. But, it's a very small market and does not seem to keep regular hours, so don't depend on it for your picnic fixin's. The Village Store at the lake itself can supply your needs.

The area you're riding through was all part of the 17,000 acre Santa Manuela Rancho granted to Francis Ziba Branch in 1837. In 1866, Branch deeded over 13,000 acres of his land to his three sons as wedding gifts. The oldest, Ramon, built an adobe home that stands today (5.5) on a tree-shaded knoll. The owners of the property, Don and Rosemary Talley, are winemakers and operate a small winery and tasting room adjacent to the adobe. Their wine label depicts the adobe guarded by towering eucalyptus trees.

22

Even if you're not ready for a stop, at least take a spin through Biddle Regional Park (6.2). Set in a densely wooded area, there are picnic facilities, restrooms and water. In fact, it's a nice picnic destination in itself. Once past Biddle Park, the hills close in and you start to feel the climb as you wind your way up to Lopez Dam (7.7). The work is rewarded, though, when you get your first look at the dark blue waters of Lopez Lake reflecting the foothills that cradle it.

The road follows the lake shoreline to Hi Mountain Road (10.5). *If you're going to take the SIDETRIP, turn right and follow the SIDETRIP directions. If not, continue straight to the park entrance (10.7).* There's a day use fee for cars, but bicyclists are admitted free. Why? According to one park ranger, "You paid your fee when you pedaled out here." Now you're on your own. Relax and enjoy. (Mileage into the lake is not included in the total mileage.)

On your return, you'll probably have to fight a headwind that gusts up the valley in the afternoon, especially in the summer. But, just as you climbed gently to the lake, you descend gently to the Village.

Follow Lopez Drive/Huasna Road to the intersection of Highway 227 (19.7/24.3) and veer to the left, following Highway 227 (Branch Street). On your left, you'll notice a one-room schoolhouse that looks slightly out of place amid the hustle and bustle of the local school district bus barn. The Santa Manuela School was built originally in 1877, then rebuilt in 1901 after a fire. It stood for more than 50 years at the fork of Lopez and Arroyo Grande Creeks near the dam in Lopez Canyon. When construction on the lake began, the schoolhouse, no longer in use, was moved to an area above the waterline. Unfortunately, vandals thoughtlessly defaced the structure. Not wanting to lose a piece of history, the South County Historical Society had the building moved to its current location in 1986. The school is open to the public on weekends and other days by appointment.

After the stop, Highway 227 leads through the Village of Arroyo Grande —a town founded in 1867 with the building of a schoolhouse and a blacksmith shop. Turn left on Mason Street (20.2/24.8) then right immediately into Olohan Alley. Voila! You're back where you started. If you have energy to spare, park your bike and take a stroll through town. There are a number of interesting historical spots including the famous and fun Swinging Bridge, a suspension footbridge built originally by William Short in the 1880s to connect his home on one side of Arroyo Grande Creek and his orchard on the other. The Village also offers good food and unique shops. And the Village Green is a great place to kick back and reflect on the day's ride.

SIDETRIP

Follow Lopez Drive to Hi Mountain Road (10.5) and turn right. The road is narrow and lightly traveled. And, although paved, it's rough. But, the area is absolutely beautiful, a valley completely surrounded by oak-covered hills. You feel like you're miles from civilization. At the Y (11.4) stay right, following the signs to Pozo. The road continues to roller-coaster to the Forest Service Station (12.4) then immediately turns to dirt. Turn around and return to Lopez Drive (15.1), turn right and proceed to the park entrance (15.3). *The second number in the parentheses represents your total mileage.*

Monarch butterflies visit the South County in fall and winter.

Windsurfers, Lopez Lake.

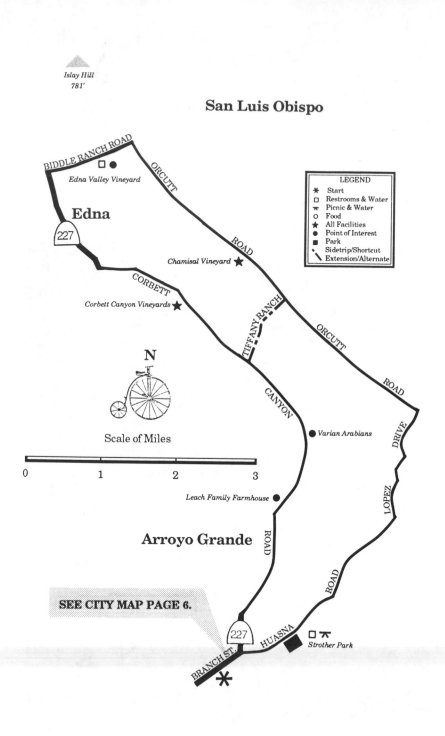

Islay Hill
781'

San Luis Obispo

BIDDLE RANCH ROAD

Edna Valley Vineyard

ORCUTT

Edna

227

ROAD

Chamisal Vineyard

CORBETT

Corbett Canyon Vineyards

TIFFANY RANCH

ORCUTT

ROAD

LEGEND
✳ Start
☐ Restrooms & Water
🍴 Picnic & Water
○ Food
★ All Facilities
● Point of Interest
■ Park
•. Sidetrip/Shortcut
\ Extension/Alternate

N

Scale of Miles

CANYON

● Varian Arabians

DRIVE

0   1   2   3

Leach Family Farmhouse ●

LOPEZ

Arroyo Grande

ROAD

ROAD

SEE CITY MAP PAGE 6.

227

HUASNA

☐ 🍴 Strother Park

BRANCH ST.

✳

4 — CORBETT CANYON
AND THE EDNA VALLEY

RIDE AT A GLANCE

DISTANCE: 20 miles
TRAFFIC: light to moderate
BIKE LANE: wide shoulder in higher traffic areas
RATING: easy to moderate
SHORTCUT: easy 14 miles with a couple of short, steep
                   "ups"on Tiffany Ranch Road

Winding country roads, oak-dotted hills, pastures filled with beautiful horses, scenic wineries surrounded by lush vineyards. Top it all off with a post-ride hot fudge sundae or a double-decker ice cream cone and this ramble through rural Arroyo Grande and the southern fringes of the city of San Luis Obispo is pure ambrosia.

You pedal past small farmhouses, large commercial ranches, elegant homes and horses, horses and more horses before visiting three of the county's fine wineries, located in the Edna Valley Viticultural Area. And, you get a glimpse of the county's history as you follow the path of the Pacific Coast Railway — a narrow gauge rail system that carried passengers and freight from Port San Luis to Los Olivos from the late 1800s to the early 1940s.

The Village of Arroyo Grande — located on the north end of Arroyo Grande Creek on the stage road from San Luis Obispo to Santa Barbara — began in 1867 with a schoolhouse and a blacksmith shop. By 1876, hotels, saloons, shops and homes had been added. The storefronts lining Branch Street today look much the same as they did when the village was young.

Start the ride in the parking lot (called Olohan Alley) behind **Ira's Bike Shop** (0.0) in the Village of Arroyo Grande (see the Arroyo Grande map at the beginning of this section). Head east, past the gazebo and Swinging Bridge, to the end of the alley (.1) and turn left on Mason Street. At the signal (.2), turn right on Branch Street. Continue on Branch (Highway 227) to the intersection of Huasna Road (.6) and veer left, following the signs to San Luis Obispo. Turn right on Corbett Canyon Road (1.1) and look for swans gliding on a pond just off the road to the right.   Now you're headed into horse country. The road is narrow with little or no shoulder, but traffic is light.   Don't miss the "gingerbready" Victorian farmhouse on the left (3.0). Built

27

in 1901, it was sold to John C. Leach in 1904. The Leach family lived in the home until 1956. The house was saved from destruction in 1962 and continues to be a private residence.

Just past Varian Arabians (4.0) — look for moms and new babies in the front pastures during the spring and summer — the road makes a gentle turn and winds through a eucalyptus grove. If you look to your right, you can see the roadbed of the Pacific Coast Railway. The rails are long gone, but the flat, level roadbed remains. In fact, much of Corbett Canyon Road lies directly on top of the old railway route.

If you're taking the SHORTCUT, turn right on Tiffany Ranch Road (5.3) and follow the SHORTCUT directions. If not, ride the roller coaster that is Corbett Canyon Road to Corbett Canyon Vineyards (6.0). Entrance to the winery and tasting room is via a long driveway on your left. (This mileage is not included in the total mileage.) Tours and tasting are available as are food, water, picnic facilities and restrooms. After your respite, continue north (left) on Corbett Canyon Road to Highway 227 (7.4) and turn right.

Highway 227 is the "back way" into San Luis Obispo from the South County and traffic can be heavy, especially in the early morning and late afternoon hours. However, there is a wide shoulder that makes for safe cycling.

The false-fronted, western-style building (8.0) — plus the original streets and a few houses — is all that remains of the town of Edna. In 1894, Lynford Maxwell filed a subdivision plan for a town he called Maxwellton. Somewhere along the line, folks decided Maxwellton was too big of a mouthful and the town was renamed Edna. No one is certain who Edna was. Some say a racehorse. Others say a German nun. Still others say she was Maxwell's daughter. But, whoever she was, her namesake prospered from the late 1880s until the early 1900s thanks, in part, to the rich asphaltum deposits around the corner in Price Canyon, the fertile land and the Pacific Coast and Southern Pacific railroads. The post office, train depot, schoolhouse, blacksmith shop and saloons are gone now, victims of progress. But, the general store remains as a reminder of the town's glory days.

Follow 227 north through the Edna Valley — a nationally recognized viticultural area — and turn right on Biddle Ranch Road (8.9). Named for John Biddle, an influential valley rancher who died in 1891, this narrow farm road passes through produce fields, vineyards and walnut groves. Don't be surprised at the low flying aircraft — San Luis Obispo County Airport is just north of here. Stop at Edna Valley Vineyard (9.5) on the right. There's tasting, tours, water and restrooms. Stay on

28

Biddle Ranch Road until it ends at Orcutt Road (10.1) and turn right, following the signs to Lopez Lake and Arroyo Grande. Orcutt Road at this point is narrow and relatively flat, lined by wide open spaces and gently rolling hills. At 11.8 miles it widens and there is a nice wide shoulder. Chamisal Vineyards and winery (12.2) is open for tours and tasting. There's also food, water and restrooms. Past Chamisal, Orcutt Road turns to rollies. A pleasant landscape with homes perched on the tops of hills here and there and cows grazing in the fields below.

At Tiffany Ranch Road (13.0), Orcutt Road narrows and the shoulder disappears. *If you opted for the SHORTCUT, this is where you rejoin the main route. The second number in the parentheses represents your total mileage.* Traffic remains light as you roll through oak-dotted hills to the Lopez Water Treatment Plant reservoir (15.0/8.1) — a pretty lake sort of affair spanning the road. At Lopez Drive (15.4/8.7), turn right.

Lopez Drive winds past small farms, ranches, walnut groves, one last horse ranch — Ka-Shatta Arabians (17.3/10.6) — and Strother Park (19.0/12.3) before it ends at the junction of Highway 227 (19.7/13.0). The one-room schoolhouse on your left was built originally in 1877 then rebuilt in 1901 following a fire. Classes were held in the school — which stood in an area near the Lopez dam spillway — until 1958 when it closed. When work began on the lake in 1969, the school was moved to a spot above the impending waterline. In 1986, the local historical society moved the structure to its present location. Members open it to the public on weekends.

Turn left on Branch (Highway 227) and follow it to Mason Street (20.2/13.5) then make an immediate right into Olohan Alley to return to your starting point (20.3/13.6). Park your bike by Ira's and head for Burnardo'z Candy Kitchen and Ice Cream Parlor (114 West Branch) for the whipped cream and cherry to top off a perfect ride.

SHORTCUT

Follow Corbett Canyon Road to Tiffany Ranch Road (5.3) and turn right. This is a roller coaster with some short, steep "ups" and some fun "downs". You pedal up and down past lovely homes, green pastures lined with white fences, a large pond filled with ducks and a small vineyard. The view at the crest of each knoll is breathtaking. Miles and miles of rolling hills and ranch land. *Turn right on Orcutt Road (6.4) and rejoin the main route at this point. The second number in the parentheses represents your total mileage.*

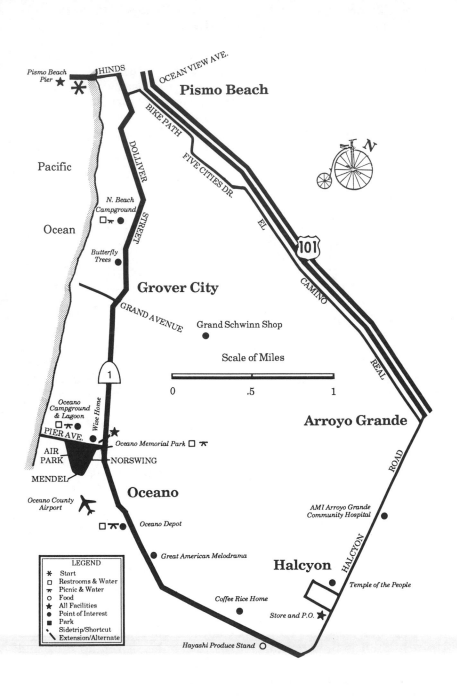

Pismo Beach Pier ★

HINDS

OCEAN VIEW AVE.

Pismo Beach

BIKE PATH

Pacific

DOLLIVER STREET

FIVE CITIES DR.

EL

Ocean

N. Beach Campground □⊼●

Butterfly Trees ●

Grover City

GRAND AVENUE

Grand Schwinn Shop ●

CAMINO

US 101

N

Scale of Miles

0   .5   1

1

Oceano Campground & Lagoon □⊼●

Wise Home

REAL

PIER AVE. ★

Oceano Memorial Park □ ⊼

AIR PARK

NORSWING

MENDEL

Arroyo Grande

Oceano County Airport ✈

Oceano

□⊼● Oceano Depot

ROAD

AMI Arroyo Grande Community Hospital ●

● Great American Melodrama

Halcyon

HALCYON

LEGEND

✳	Start
□	Restrooms & Water
⊼	Picnic & Water
○	Food
★	All Facilities
●	Point of Interest
■	Park
⋰	Sidetrip/Shortcut
＼	Extension/Alternate

Temple of the People ●

Coffee Rice Home ●

Store and P.O. ★

Hayashi Produce Stand ○

5 — PISMO BEACH, OCEANO AND HALCYON

RIDE AT A GLANCE

DISTANCE: 11 miles
TRAFFIC: moderate
BIKE LANE: yes, on Highway 1 through Pismo Beach
RATING: easy

Seagulls roosting on pier pilings. Thousands of butterflies clustered on eucalyptus boughs. Ducks floating on a placid pond. Beaver busy building dams. They're all part of this easy pedal, perfect for families. So, pack a lunch — don't forget a bag of bread crumbs for the ducks — and head for Pismo Beach.

Pismo Beach is part of the original 8,838 acre Rancho Pizmo owned by John Price. The town was laid out by the Pismo Beach Company in 1887 and founded in 1891 when the Southern Pacific Railroad completed the last link of the coast route from San Luis Obispo to Santa Barbara. In 1907, a large dance pavillion was built where the pier parking lot stands today. The town already had an inn, a small hotel, a bathhouse, skating rink and a large tent city as well as several saloons and a growing reputation for fun and entertainment. The pavillion burned down in the early 1940s and owner Joe Rose replaced it with a ballroom called the Rose Garden. Today that building, located next to the pier on Pomeroy Avenue, is part of a shopping mall.

Start the ride in the pier parking lot (see the Pismo Beach map at the beginning of this section). There are public restrooms here and a number of shopping, eating and entertainment possibilities. And, of course, there's the pier — a perfect place to stroll and people-watch. Pismo's original wharf, built by the Meherin brothers in 1881, collapsed in a heavy storm in the mid-1890s. The new pier was dedicated on July 4, 1924. It has been battered and repaired many times since, but remains the center of activity in this seaside town.

Exit the parking lot with a left turn on Hinds Avenue (0.0) and turn right on Dolliver Street (.1). The Chamber of Commerce is on your right as you make the turn. Dolliver is Highway 1 as it goes through Pismo Beach. It can be quite busy on weekends and during the summer, but the road is wide and there is a marked bicycle lane. Continue south past the North Beach Campground (.8), a part of Pismo State Beach.

Just past the entrance to the campground is a large grove of eucalyptus trees (1.1). From October through early spring, these

31

trees are filled with thousands of Monarch butterflies. Scientists believe the fragile creatures travel across the Rocky Mountains and the Sierra Nevada range from as far away as Canada to winter in the balmy Pismo Beach climate.

You can lock your bike to the fence near the road or walk it back in with you. Follow the marked trail to the trees. If it's cool, look carefully. Hanging in clusters with wings folded back, the butterflies are perfectly camouflaged. Once you spot them, the sheer numbers are enough to bring butterflies to your stomach. And, when they take flight ... well, it's like watching shafts of sunlight filter through tiny, stained glass windows.

The docents from the Morro Bay Museum of Natural History give free interpretative talks at the Butterfly Trees on Saturdays and Sundays during the fall and winter. For more information on the walks, check the information kiosk in the grove or ask the ranger at the entrance to the state park.

When you leave the Butterfly Trees, continue south on Highway 1. At Grand Avenue (1.6) the highway narrows and the official bike lane ends. Our ride continues south but, if you're riding fat tires, you may want to detour to the right on Grand Avenue and try a spin on the wide, hard-packed "driving" beach. Cars have to pay a dollar or two for the privilege, but bicycles go free. (If you're in need of a bike shop, turn left on Grand Avenue. **Grand Schwinn Shop** is just .6 miles up on the corner of 10th Street and Grand Avenue.)

Back on track, the highway roller-coasters past more of Pismo State Beach on the right and the Southern Pacific railroad tracks and RV parks on the left. At 2.3 miles you enter the town of Oceano.

Like Pismo Beach, Oceano has a colorful past. With the coming of the Southern Pacific Railroad (Oceano got the depot), subdividers decided it was time to build year-round beach colonies. Colonization began in Oceano in 1895 when developers dredged a freshwater lagoon, laid a spur track to the site and built a large, two-story dance pavillion. The pavillion, which stood on the beach just south of the Oceano ramp on Pier Avenue, was surrounded on three sides by 1000 lots with 25 and 30 foot frontages. It opened on August 5, 1895 with a gala free clambake.

The Oceano pavillion outlasted its sister in Pismo Beach. In fact, there are tales of bootleg liquor being stashed there during the Prohibition era. But, in the 1950s it was finally condemned and torn down. The waterfront community never got off the ground and in 1935 Harold E. Guiton, one of the developers, donated 4.8 acres of lagoon property to the State Park System and encouraged others to sell adjoining land to the state. The result, Pismo State Beach's Oceano Campground.

Turn right on Pier Avenue (2.6), following the signs to the Oceano Campground. There's a market on the left and a retaurant on the right. On the northeast corner of Norswing (2.7) is an elaborate Moorish-looking home. It was built by W.A. Wise, a San Francisco land promoter, during Oceano's heyday.

Turn left on Norswing. The Oceano Memorial Park, a part of the San Luis Obispo County Park System, is on your right. There's a wonderful expanse of lawn that sweeps down to a duck-filled lake. Stop, get your bag of bread crumbs out and go to it. The ducks are anything but shy. If you brought a picnic lunch, this is the ideal place to stop. There are restrooms, picnic tables and barbecues as well as water fountains and a children's playground.

Leave the park via Norswing and turn right on Mendel Drive (2.9). Directly ahead is the Oceano Airport — a great place to stop and watch small plane activity. Loop the lake by turning right on Air Park Drive (3.0) and right again on Pier Avenue (3.1). (To the left is the Oceano beach ramp and the site of the Oceano Pavillion. There are also a number of eateries and novelty shops.)

The entrance to the Oceano Campground is at 3.2 miles. The Oceano Lagoon is encompassed within the campground. Stop and take the easy one mile hike along the Harold Guiton Trail that circles the lagoon. (Mileage into the park is not included in the total mileage.) If you're lucky, you may see a beaver working on his dam. Beaver were introduced to the lagoon in the 1930s by sportsmen. At that time, the State Park System thought it should provide hunting experiences for its visitors. That's no longer the case, of course, but the beaver remain and have multiplied.

Turn left as you leave the campground, return to Highway 1 (3.4), and turn right. The Oceano Depot (3.9) was restored through the efforts of Harold Guiton, Jr. — son of the man who donated his lagoon property to the state. The building serves as a community center and houses a museum of railroad and local history memorabilia.

There are many markets and restaurants in Oceano. And, there's the Great American Melodrama (4.2). If you have time one evening during your stay, don't miss the chance to cheer the hero and boo the villain. It's pure family entertainment — staged by professional singers, dancers and comedians — complete with popcorn and hot dogs.

Highway 1 makes a sharp curve to the left (4.3) as it leaves "downtown" Oceano and wends its way through a mixture of homes, mobile home parks and produce fields. At the intersection of the Highway and 25th Street (4.9) is the Coffee

33

Rice House, a stately Victorian surrounded by a mobile home park. Built for $11,000 in 1885, the house has three stories and 20 rooms and every embellishment, turret and minaret imaginable. During its peak, the grounds included a paddock, racetrack and various outbuildings. When Rice became financially discouraged and left Oceano, the house was bought by Francis A. LaDue and Dr. William H. Dower, leaders of a theosophical society who were in the process of moving their headquarters from Syracuse, New York to Arroyo Grande — more specifically, Halcyon. They used it as a hotel for followers and later for a sanatorium. During that time, the mansion was surrounded by lovely landscaped grounds. The sanatorium closed in the 1920s and the house was sold. But Dower, LaDue and their followers remained. Today, the quiet, tree-lined town of Halcyon is the international headquarters of the movement.

Just up the street is Hayashi Produce Stand (5.2). It's a great place to stop for fresh fruit and veggies. During strawberry season, people drive (or bicycle!) for miles to purchase the sweet, red berries grown in the fields surrounding the stand.

Turn left on Halcyon Road (5.4) and take some time to visit the town of Halcyon (5.8). The quiet streets are perfect for pedaling. There's a country store and post office. And, of course, the Temple of the People. The temple was built between 1922 and 1924. Architecturally, it is based on an equilateral triangle with sides curved to symbolize the heart. Made of white stucco, it has 13 pillars on each side, seven doors and 26 windows, each containing a square within a square. Inside, the building is 49 feet long from corner to corner. The three great roof beams converge in the center, directly above one of two altars, with a triangular light in the apex.

Adjacent to the temple is the Halcyon University Center. This building is open to the public by appointment (call 489-2822) and contains a magnificent collection of paintings by Harold Forgostein, Guardian-in-Chief of the Temple. The huge canvasses depict the life of Hiawatha, an Indian leader who welded five warring tribes into the powerful Iroquois Nation. The motto of the Temple is: "Creeds disappear, hearts remain." True to its name, Halcyon is a place of calm, peace and tranquility.

When you leave Halcyon (the mileage into the town is not included in the total mileage), turn left on Halcyon Road. Traffic will pick up a bit as you head towards Arroyo Grande. By the time you reach Grand Avenue (6.9), it can be quite heavy. Halcyon ends at El Camino Real (7.2). Turn left and follow this freeway frontage road back to Pismo Beach. There are a number of gas stations and restaurants along the way. When you get to

34

Temple of the People, Halcyon.

Bob's Big Boy in the Five Cities Shopping Center (the frontage road and the parking lot become one and the same at this point), follow the road to the right and then, at the stop sign marking the freeway entrance, veer to the left and go up on the bike path that runs along the edge of the freeway. You'll be facing northbound traffic, but are guarded by a concrete wall. The bike path ends at Ocean View Avenue (10.2). Exit very carefully. It's a tight squeeze and you can't see on-coming bike or pedestrian traffic. Follow Ocean View Avenue to Dolliver Street (10.3) and turn right. Then make the left at Hinds Avenue (10.5) and return to the pier parking lot (10.6).

If you haven't done so already, take time to stroll the pier. Watch the fishermen, the surfers, the gulls. Enjoy the fresh ocean breeze and the magnificent view that takes in everything from Avila Beach in the north to Point Sal in the south. And, remember, those creaky old planks you're walking on are a piece of Pismo Beach history.

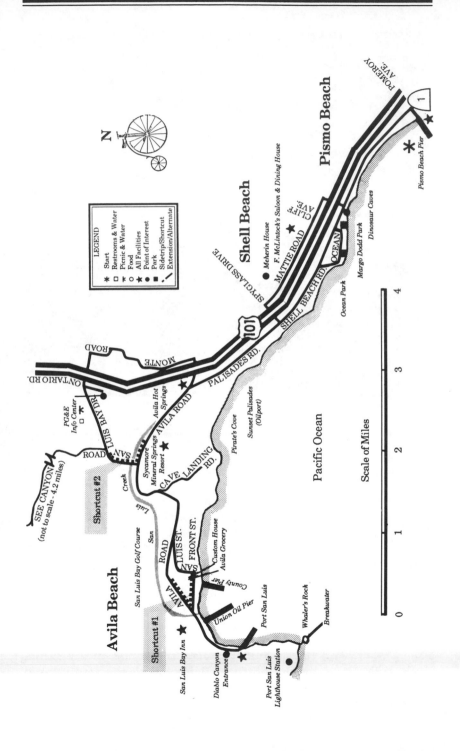

6 — AVILA BEACH AND SEE CANYON

RIDE AT A GLANCE

DISTANCE: 29 miles
TRAFFIC: light to moderate
BIKE LANE: yes, on Highway 1 in Pismo Beach; decent
                     shoulder in heavier traffic areas
RATING: easy to moderate
SHORTCUT #1:   easy 16 miles to Avila Beach and back
SHORTCUT #2:   easy 21 miles to See Canyon and back

If you like white sandy beaches, cotton candy, girls in bikinis and guys in jams and the funky surf shops, eateries and curio shops that fronted beaches in the 1940s and '50s, you're going to love this ride. If you like the peace and quiet of a lightly-traveled country road and the crunch of an apple just off the tree, you're going to love this ride. If you like to eat, you're going to love this ride. If you like the challenge of out-sprinting farm dogs, you're going to love this ride. No matter what you like, a pedal out to Avila Beach and See Canyon is pure pleasure.

Start the ride in the the parking lot at the Pismo Beach pier (see the Pismo Beach map at the beginning of this section). At the turn-of-the-century, vacation tent cabins, an amusement park and a dance pavillion occupied this area. People came from near and far to enjoy Pismo's unique hospitality. The structures are gone now — victims of fire and progress — but Pismo Beach has retained its reputation for relaxation and unbridled fun.

Exit the parking lot with a right turn on Pomeroy Avenue (0.0). Turn left on Dolliver Street (.1), then left again on Price Street (.6).

At 1.9 miles on the left is what is known as the Dinosaur Caves area. In Pismo Beach's heyday, the multi-colored caverns deep in the bowels of the cliffs were a great tourist attraction. Known then as the Shell Beach Caverns, the site was guarded by a giant cement dinosaur. Unfortunately, the dinosaur was never completed and he remained headless until, like the caverns, he collapsed. The caves were sealed off many years ago, but the name Dinosaur Caves lingers.

At 2.0 miles you enter the town of Shell Beach and Price Street becomes Shell Beach Road. Prior to the 1930s, Shell Beach was nothing but pea fields. Then a realtor bought the property and began selling lots to residents of the San Joaquin Valley who built weekend and summer homes. After World War II, the complexion of the neighborhood changed from resort to

37

Pismo Beach pier at sunset.

residential. Today, the small town is actually an incorporated part of Pismo Beach, but residents prefer the Shell Beach designation. (If you'd like to detour to the beach, turn left on Cliff Avenue to get to Margo Dodd Park or Vista Del Mar Avenue to get to Ocean Park.)

Continue on Shell Beach Road. Once past Spyglass Drive (3.4), you get your first glimpse of San Luis Bay and Avila Beach. Sunset Palisades (4.2), a cliffside residential area, was once known as Oilport. Touted as the major port from which oil from the Santa Maria region would flow around the world, the modern port and refinery opened for business in August, 1907 and was destroyed by a tidal wave in December of that same year. Houses began making an appearance after World War II and today the area is known for its luxury homes.

After Sunset Palisades, Shell Beach Road becomes Palisades Road. Turn left on Avila Road (4.8) and zip downhill to Avila Hot Springs (5.0), a resort that dates back to 1907 when a well drilled for oil yielded warm artesian water. The landowners capitalized on the find and built a swimming pool and bathhouse. Since that day, people have come to the Springs to "take the waters". Celebrity guests include Charlie Chaplin, W.C. Fields and Rudolph Valentino who enjoyed a soak on their way to visit Randolph Hearst in San Simeon. The Springs' reputation was a bit shady during the days of Prohibition, but

38

today it's a place for family fun. There's a swimming pool, hot tubs, snack bar and campground. And restrooms, water and picnic facilities are available.

After the hot springs, stay left at the fork, following Avila Road and the signs to Port San Luis. Sycamore Mineral Springs Resort (5.6), nestled on the hillside, began in 1886. You can soak in the resort's *al fresco* sulphur-based hot tubs 24 hours a day. Or, take a swim in the public pool. There's also a therapeutic massage center if your bike-weary bod is in need of some TLC.

If you're going to take SHORTCUT #2, turn right at San Luis Bay Drive (6.0) and follow the SHORTCUT #2 directions. If you're doing the complete ride or SHORTCUT #1, continue straight. At 6.7 miles, Cave Landing Road goes off to the left. It's a steep climb to an area known locally as Pirate's Cove. Tradition has it that pirates — and later rum-runners — approached the landing under cover of fog or night and stashed their illicit cargo in a large cave above the waterline. In 1860, David Mallagh, an Irish sea captain, built a wharf here. For years, he handled all the trade which came to San Luis Bay and operated the only stage line between the landing and San Luis Obispo. Today Pirate's Cove has the dubious honor of being the area's clothing-optional beach.

After Cave Landing Road, Avila Road climbs past the San Luis Bay Golf Course. Turn left on San Luis Street (7.1) and follow it to Front Street (7.5) and turn right. Voilà! You're in Avila Beach, a 1940s- and '50s-style beach town.

Avila — renamed Avila Beach in 1962 — is part of the 22,136 acre San Miguelito Rancho granted to Don Miguel Avila in 1842. Like all rancheros, the Avilas suffered heavily during the drought of 1863-1864. In 1867, in an effort to recoup some of their losses, they laid out the town which bears their name and sold lots to settlers and businessmen.

When John Harford built People's Wharf (located about a block south of today's county or downtown pier) in 1868, Avila began to prosper. But, it was Harford's second wharf, built at the western end of the bay, and the narrow gauge railway — that ran 70 miles from Avila to Los Olivos — that put Avila on the map.

Several of the town's original buildings are still standing. The Old Custom House, now a restaurant, was just that — a customs point for people and freight coming into Port Harford. The restaurant is very popular with locals. Breakfast, lunch and dinner are served, but my favorite is breakfast or Sunday brunch on the patio. Next door is the Avila Grocery & Mercantile, the oldest continuously operating business in town. Built in 1917, it's an Avila Beach institution and features a complete deli.

The county pier (7.7) was built in 1917. It lost a chunk out of the middle during the big storms of 1983, but was repaired, to the relief of gulls and fishermen. There are public restrooms at the foot of the pier plus water, a playground and a sandy beach.

Continue through Avila Beach to Avila Road (7.9). *If you're taking SHORTCUT #1, turn right and follow the SHORTCUT #1 directions. If not, turn left.* The bridge you cross immediately after the left turn was built in 1968. It replaced the old Pacific Coast Railway bridge which served trains until the 1940s and then automobiles until it was condemned in the late 1960s. There were plans to restore the old bridge which spanned the creek just to the west of the new bridge. In fact, it was hoped that it could be a bicycle path. Unfortunately, it toppled before restoration got underway.

Avila Road follows the roadbed of the Pacific Coast Railway from Avila Beach to Port San Luis. The San Luis Bay Inn (8.0), built in 1968 as a private resort, is today open to the public. In addition to hotel accommodations, there's a golf course, tennis courts and a restaurant — Sunday brunch here is wonderful — with a fabulous view of Port San Luis and the bay.

The Union Oil pier (8.1) was originally built in 1914 by the Pacific Coast Railroad Company. Union Oil paid royalties for the use of this pipeline wharf until 1940 when it purchased it. The wooden pier was completely destroyed by raging surf in 1983 and was rebuilt of steel and concrete.

Just past the entrance to the Diablo Canyon Nuclear Power Plant (9.0), Avila Road swings left into Port San Luis. Formerly Port Harford, this pier, built in 1873 by John Harford, was the terminus of the Pacific Coast Railway. From here, passengers and cargo were loaded aboard steamships bound for San Francisco. During the port's glory days there were two whaling stations — one on the island still known as Whaler's Rock at the end of the breakwater and the other on a secluded beach near where the lighthouse stands today — and the luxurious Hotel Marre guarded the port entrance.

Today, Port San Luis is a working and pleasure harbor. There are public restrooms, showers, a marine supply store, a fish market, two restaurants and a seafood snack bar. Ride out to the end of the pier (this mileage is not included in the totals) for a good look at the breakwater — built in 1913 from rock quarried from Morro Rock — and the Port San Luis Lighthouse Station. Built in 1890, the light first ran on whale oil, then coal oil and now electricity. In 1975, the light and accompanying fog horn were automated and the station was deactivated by the Coast Guard. Local historians hope the station, which has been the subject of much vandalism, can be restored and used as a maritime museum or a youth hostel. The Olde Port Inn — the

40

pier-end restaurant and fish market — occupies the building which served as a warehouse for the Pacific Coast Company.

Exit the port (9.4), backtrack to San Luis Bay Drive (12.5), turn left, then left again at See Canyon Road (13.0).

There's a local myth that Mary See — of See's Candy fame — is the sister of Joseph See who settled in and named the canyon in 1850. See's public relations department won't substantiate the claim. But, it won't discount it either. So, local residents continue to recount the story.

The ride back into See Canyon is marvelous any time of year. The road roller-coasters and climbs gently along a tributary of San Luis Creek. At first, oaks and sycamores crowd the pavement and offer shade, then the landscape opens up and apple orchards take their place. See Canyon has been a major apple-producing area since the early 1900s. There are about six family-run orchards that sell apples and fresh cider from roadside stands during the season — usually late August through October. If you're riding in the canyon during this time of year, be sure to leave room in your panniers for apples. In addition to apples, you can also buy honey, nuts and other fresh goodies in season.

Black Walnut Road (17.2) is a good place to turn around. If you like to climb, though, you might want to continue on See Canyon Road until it turns to dirt (you climb 800 feet in 1.5 miles). Or, if you're riding fat tires, you may want to follow the road all the way to San Luis Obispo. If you opt to do that, at the summit you get a wonderful view of Morro Bay, San Luis Obispo and everything in between.

The ride out of the canyon is downhill all the way. Enjoy your flight, then turn left on San Luis Bay Drive (21.3). The hill immediately ahead looks worse than it is. It peaks at 21.7 miles and, at 22.0 miles, you start a fast descent. San Luis Bay Drive crosses Ontario Road at 22.1 miles. If you'd like to tour the Pacific Gas and Electric Information Center, turn right. There are exhibits and films that explain the Diablo Canyon operation along with picnic facilities and restrooms. If not, continue straight. The road crosses the freeway then ends at Monte Road (22.4) where you turn right.

Monte Road is pure delight. Green pastures, black and white cows, woodsmoke curling from farmhouse chimneys, golden haystacks, decaying barns, churning windmills and no traffic. Turn right at the wooden bridge (22.8). From here the road roller-coasters through pastures framed by oak-dotted hills and over several metal cattle crossings. Don't be surprised if you're chased by a farm dog or two. They're friendly, but they love to play the game.

41

Apple time, See Canyon.

Turn left *very carefully* at the frontage road (23.7) — which serves as the on-ramp for northbound freeway traffic — then right at Avila Road (23.9) and left at Palisades Road (24.0). At Spyglass Drive (25.3) turn left, cross under the freeway, then turn right on Mattie Road (25.4).

The white house with the green trim (26.4) was built in 1905 at a cost of $4,000 by Mike Meherin, the man responsible for building the first wharf in Pismo Beach in 1881. It was moved to its present location — at a cost of $4,000 — when the freeway came through.

If you're hungry, stop at F. McLintock's Saloon and Dining House (26.6), perhaps the most famous eatery in San Luis Obispo County. Huge steaks, skillets of fried potatoes, beans, salsa and fresh bread and salad are complemented by excellent service and a relaxing western atmosphere. The restaurant opened in 1973. Many years prior to that, the building housed Mattie's, a gambling and pleasure saloon owned by Mattie Smyer, Pismo Beach's colorful madam. Although the restaurant still retains some of the original artifacts from its earlier and wilder days, today it caters to families.

After McLintock's, Mattie Road descends and crosses under the freeway. Turn left on Price Street/Shell Beach Road (27.6), right on Dolliver Street (28.2) and right again on Pomeroy Avenue (28.7) to return to the pier (28.8).

If you have some energy left, a stroll on the pier is definitely in order. Or, you might want to park your bike and explore Pismo Beach. Complete with eateries, shopping and fun, it's still a mecca for landlocked tourists.

SHORTCUT #1

Follow the main route to Front Street in Avila Beach. At the intersection of Front Street and Avila Road (7.9), turn right and backtrack to Pismo Beach via Avila Road, Palisades/Shell Beach Road, Dolliver Street and Pomeroy Avenue.

SHORTCUT #2

Follow the main route to San Luis Bay Drive (6.0) and turn right. Turn left at See Canyon Road (6.5) and ride into the canyon to Black Walnut Road (10.7). Turn around, exit the canyon at San Luis Bay Drive (14.9), turn right and return to Avila Road (15.4). Turn left and backtrack to Pismo Beach via Avila Road, Palisades/Shell Beach Road, Dolliver Street and Pomeroy Avenue.

43

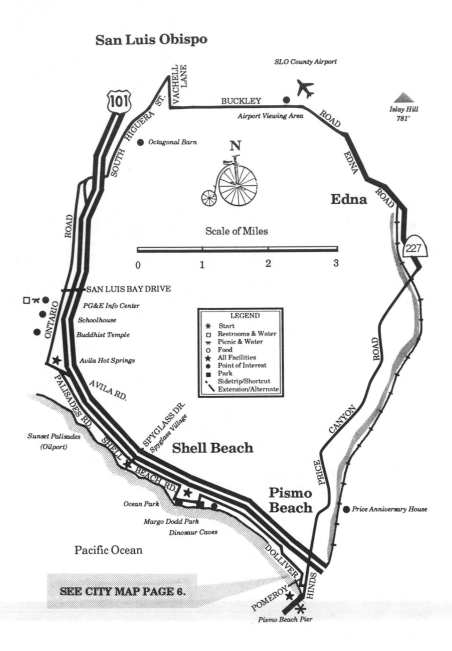

San Luis Obispo

SLO County Airport

BUCKLEY
Airport Viewing Area

Islay Hill
781'

Octagonal Barn

N

Edna

Scale of Miles

0   1   2   3

101

SOUTH HIGUERA ST.

VACHELL LANE

ROAD

EDNA ROAD

ONTARIO ROAD

227

SAN LUIS BAY DRIVE
PG&E Info Center
Schoolhouse
Buddhist Temple

Avila Hot Springs

AVILA RD.

LEGEND	
*	Start
□	Restrooms & Water
⊼	Picnic & Water
○	Food
★	All Facilities
●	Point of Interest
■	Park
⋮	Sidetrip/Shortcut
⟍	Extension/Alternate

PALISADES RD.

SHELL BEACH RD.

SPYGLASS DR.
Spyglass Village

Shell Beach

Sunset Palisades
(Oilport)

Ocean Park

Margo Dodd Park

Dinosaur Caves

Pismo Beach

Price Anniversary House

CANYON ROAD

PRICE

DOLLIVER

POMEROY

HINDS

Pacific Ocean

SEE CITY MAP PAGE 6.

Pismo Beach Pier

7 — SAN LUIS OBISPO COUNTY AIRPORT AND AVILA HOT SPRINGS

RIDE AT A GLANCE

DISTANCE:	22 miles
TRAFFIC:	light to moderate
BIKE LANE:	wide shoulder in higher traffic areas
RATING:	easy to moderate

Next to cycling, I love flying. I'll fly in anything — ultralights, hot air balloons, small fixed-wing craft, helicopters, jetliners. I'm not particular. If it can get off the ground, I'm game. And, if I can't fly in 'em, I love to watch 'em take off and land.

If you share my enthusiasm for armchair flying, this ride is for you. You get a "runway center" seat at the San Luis Obispo County Airport, plus a leisurely pedal through some of the county's more pleasant rural areas. Add to that a relaxing soak in a bubbling hot spring and this loop is a great way to spend a morning or afternoon.

The ride begins and ends in Pismo Beach, once known as the Clam Capital of the World. Before 1920, clams were in great abundance here. But the continual impact of hordes of clammers, often taking thousands each day, depleted the supply. In those days, farmers plowed the sand, turned up the bivalves, and fed them to their chickens and hogs. Clamming is still popular in Pismo Beach, but the days when huge clams "paved the beach" are gone.

Start in the pier parking lot (see the Pismo Beach map at the beginning of this section) and exit with a left turn on Hinds Avenue (0.0). The Chamber of Commerce is on the southwest corner of Hinds and Dolliver (.1). It's easy to spot; it's the building with the giant cement clam out front. Stay on Hinds. After you cross Highway 101 (.3), the name changes to Price Canyon Road.

Price Canyon is named for John Michael Price, owner of 7,000 acres of the original 8,838 acre Rancho Pizmo granted in 1840 to Jose Ortega. Ortega sold the land to Isaac Sparks in 1866. Sparks, in turn, sold portions to Price and David P. Mallagh.

In 1893, Price built a three-gabled frame house as a gift for his wife on their 50th anniversary. Known as the "Anniversary House", it still stands and can be seen at the base of the hills

45

directly behind the Pacific Gas and Electric yard (.7). The adobes and barns which were part of the homestead have crumbled, but the South County Historical Society and the City of Pismo Beach have joined forces to restore the wooden home. Eventually it will house a museum, surrounded by a park.

Price Canyon Road roller-coasters through oak-covered hills, pastures filled with grazing cows and several cuts in the rocky hillsides which ooze oil and tar. It's known that the Chumash Indians used these oil deposits as long ago as 7000 B.C. In fact, the name Pismo is derived from the Chumash "pizmu" or tar. In the 1880s, 100 tons of asphaltum a month were shipped from Price Canyon to San Francisco via the Pacific Coast Railway and Steamship Company to be used for street paving. Later, furnaces were set up in the canyon to melt the tar out of the bituminous rock. Oil production is still prominent in the canyon.

Turn left *carefully* onto Highway 227 (5.2). This is a busy road — it's the "back way" into San Luis Obispo from the South County — but there is a wide shoulder. At 5.4 miles, you'll notice a row of rural mailboxes and an old, false-fronted building off to the left. This is the town of Edna. Once part of the Corral de Piedra Rancho, then the site of a prosperous dairy farming operation, Edna was in its heyday during the the 1880s, 1890s and early 1900s. There was a mercantile topped by a dance hall (the western-style, sheet metal building you see from the road), a train depot, a one-room schoolhouse, a post office, a blacksmith shop and, thanks to the asphaltum mines just around the corner, three or four saloons.

Today Edna is just a wide spot in the road, its fate sealed by the development of the automobile and roads. The train made its last stop at the Edna depot in April, 1958. In 1977, the tracks, which once carried travelers and cargo to and from Edna, were bypassed.

Highway 227 runs through the Edna Valley, an area dotted with old farmhouses, new housing developments, pastures and vineyards. Wine grapes were first planted in this area prior to 1800 on Mission San Luis Obispo land. Other small plantings were made in the early 1900s. In 1968, a county farm advisor planted an experimental plot of premium varietal wine grapes on the Righetti Ranch. As a result of his experiment, several hundred acres of vineyards were planted in the valley starting in 1973. In 1982, the Edna Valley was designated an official viticultural area by the U.S. Treasury's Bureau of Alcohol, Tobacco and Firearms.

At 7.7 miles you drop down a small knoll and get a great view of the San Luis Obispo County Airport off to the left. To the

46

right is Islay Hill (it has a beacon on top), the first in the series of nine volcanic peaks that stretch from San Luis Obsipo to Morro Bay. Turn left on Buckley Road (8.0) and ride this narrow farm road to the airport viewing area (8.5).

The large tan building directly across the runway is the airport terminal. The smaller gray one next to it is the Spirit of San Luis Restaurant. Housed in the original terminal building, the restaurant serves lunch, dinner and weekend brunch. My favorite spot is the patio right next to the runway. (If you'd like to visit the airport or eat in the restaurant, the entrance is on Highway 227 about 1/2 mile past Buckley Road.)

When you tire of watching planes, head west (right) on Buckley Road which, at 10.6 miles, makes a sharp curve to the right and becomes Vachell Lane. Stay on Vachell to South Higuera Street (11.1) and make a very hard left. You're now headed back toward the South County.

South Higuera Street follows San Luis Creek through cow-filled pastures. The road is flat and wide with a marked shoulder and the pedaling is easy. Not much is known about the octagonal barn you pass (11.6), except that it was built before 1900 and used by the Santa Fe Dairy for milking cows. Today's owner uses it for hay storage. It's covered with white-washed boards, has a concrete floor and foundations and is roughly 32 feet on a side and 77 feet between parallel sides.

At 12.8 miles South Higuera Street curves to the right and passes under the freeway. Once under the freeway, turn right on the frontage road (there's a bike route sign to mark the way). You're now on Ontario Road, which roller-coasters between steep hills and the freeway.

Cross San Luis Bay Drive (15.0). At the Pacific Gas and Electric Company Energy Information Center (15.1) there are a number of displays and films which discuss the coastal area and Diablo Canyon Nuclear Power Plant. And, of course, rest-rooms and water are available. Outside are tree-shaded picnic tables.

Continue south on Ontario Road. There's an old schoolhouse (15.6) then the road leading to the San Luis Obispo Buddhist Temple (15.8). The original temple, dating back to 1929, was located on the Madonna Road interchange in San Luis Obispo until the freeway right-of-way forced its removal. The new temple was built in 1962.

Ontario Road crosses San Luis Creek then ends at Avila Road (16.1) where you turn left. The baths at Avila Hot Springs (16.1) have been bubbling for more than 4,000 years. The Chumash were the first known to "take the waters". Then, in 1907, when a well drilled for oil yielded a pure artesian flow of

130 degrees, a bathhouse and swimming pool were built. People came by horse and buggy, train, steamship and later by car to soak and relax. Some of Hollywood's finest — including Rudolph Valentino, Charlie Chaplin and W.C. Fields — stopped over on their way to visit Randolph Hearst at his "ranch" in San Simeon. During the days of Prohibition, rum runners at Avila pier and Pirate's Cove smuggled cases of liquor into the back rooms of the hot springs. These were divided up by bootleggers and shipped via Highway 101 to Los Angeles and San Francisco. Girls and gambling followed and the Springs soon became *the* place to party on the Central Coast. Today, Avila Hot Springs caters to families. In addition to the swimming pool and hot tubs, there's a snack bar and campground. Restrooms, water and picnic facilities are also available.

After your soak, get back on Avila Road, sprint up a short hill and turn right on Palisades Road (16.3). You climb just a bit more and then, at 16.6 miles, get a beautiful view of the Pacific Ocean and the Sunset Palisades area.

Back in 1907, this area was known as Oilport. Proclaimed as the major port from which oil from the Santa Maria region would flow around the world, the project was built with British and American money. An eight-inch pipeline capable of carrying 25,000 barrels of oil daily from the Santa Maria fields was laid to the refinery and from there lines ran along a half-mile wharf where oil was loaded aboard tankers.

Oilport's history was short. It began operation in August, 1907 and was destroyed by a freak tidal wave on December 9 of that same year. Attempts to repair and revive the port and refinery were unsuccessful and, eventually, all the buildings and tanks were dismantled and moved.

Continue south on Palisades Road which becomes Shell Beach Road. Cross Spyglass Drive (17.7). Spyglass Village has a great deli plus a cookie shop and a drugstore. Restrooms and water are also available here.

Once past Spyglass, you enter the small community of Shell Beach. Turn right on Vista Del Mar (18.4) and zip downhill to the bluffs overlooking the ocean. At the stop sign (18.7), turn left on Ocean Boulevard. There's a nice beach with stair access at Vista Del Mar Avenue and between Morro and Cuyama Avenues. Plus, there's a small park with picnic tables and water. There are also cliffside benches where you can sit and watch the waves, the otters, the gulls and the seals.

In 1926, Floyd Calvert bought 41 acres of pea fields bordered by the ocean and the highway to the east and west and Placentia and Capistrano Avenues to the north and south. The price: $45,000. Calvert sold lots in the area for as little as $195 to

San Joaquin Valley residents who built weekend and summer cottages. After World War II, Shell Beach changed from a resort area to a residential community, thanks, in part, to soldiers who had trained in the county and wanted to live here. According to Calvert, the area was named Shell Beach by the Chumash who held their annual conclave in the area. While the men met, the women gathered shells and made jewelry.

The English Tudor-style home perched on the cliffs (18.9) — complete with windmill and lighthouse — belongs to Clifford Chapman, a San Luis Obispo businessman. Originally owned by Arthur Rogers, a Bakersfield oilman, the house was 12 years in the making. Work began in 1928 and the home was finally complete and ready for occupancy in 1940. But Rogers and his wife only used it as a weekend cottage until 1945 when they moved to Shell Beach permanently.

Chapman bought the house in 1963 after it had been empty for three years. At that time it was run down and dilapidated and local residents considered it an eye-sore beyond restoration. As you can see, they were definitely wrong.

Turn left on Placentia Avenue (19.0). The large Spanish style house on the right before you make the turn belonged to Mattie Smyer, Pismo Beach's famous madam and the owner of Mattie's Restaurant (now McLintock's). At Shell Beach Road (19.4), turn right.

At 19.6 miles on the right is an area known as Dinosaur Caves. The seaside caverns were quite a tourist attraction during Pismo Beach's heyday. According to an old advertising pamphlet, the caves were formed of very old river sediment, twisted by earthquakes and infused with lava. The sea worked on the rocks and, by the time man came along to enjoy them, the caverns were filled with multi-colored rocks. Unfortunately, one night they collapsed and the area was sealed off. Oh, the dinosaur? Well, it seems that some enterprising soul thought a giant cement dinosaur perched on the cliff at the cavern entrance would draw attention to the caves. That project was never completed, and the headless beast stood guard until, like the caves, it collapsed.

Continue south on Shell Beach Road/Price Street, turn right on Dolliver Street (21.1) and right again on Pomeroy Avenue (21.5) to return to the pier (21.6).

If time permits, take a stroll on the pier or just sit and watch the surfers and gulls. The original pier, built in 1881, collapsed in a heavy storm in the mid-1890s. The new pier was dedicated on July 4, 1924. It has been battered and repaired many times. In 1985, the wood pilings were replaced with steel. Today, the pier remains the center of Pismo Beach activity.

49

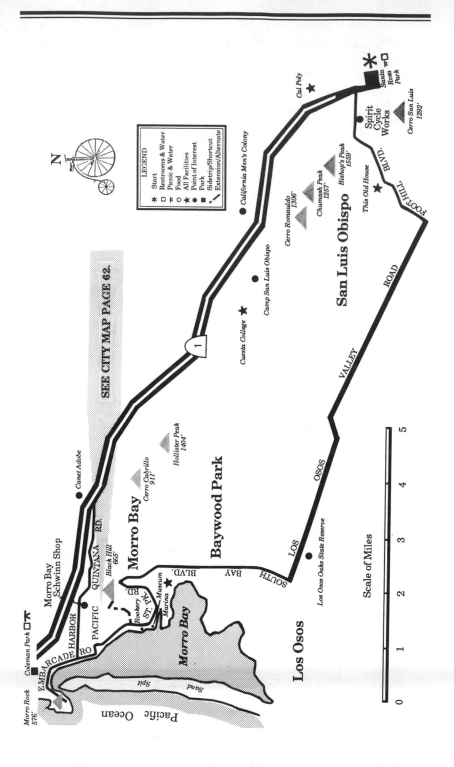

SEE CITY MAP PAGE 62.

LEGEND
* Start
□ Restrooms & Water
🍴 Picnic & Water
○ Food
● All Facilities
■ Point of Interest
■ Park
. Sidetrip/Shortcut
./ Extension/Alternate

N

Morro Rock 576'

Coleman Park

EMBARCADERO RD

Morro Bay Schwinn Shop

Canet Adobe

PACIFIC

QUINTANA RD.

HARBOR

Black Hill 665'

Rookery

ST. PK. RD.

Marina

Museum

Morro Bay

BAY BLVD.

Sand Spit

Spit

Pacific Ocean

Morro Bay

Cerro Cabrillo 911'

Hollister Peak 1404'

Baywood Park

Los Osos

Los Osos Oaks State Reserve

SOUTH BAY BLVD.

LOS OSOS VALLEY ROAD

1

Cuesta College ★

California Men's Colony ●

Camp San Luis Obispo ●

Cerro Romauldo 1306'

Chumash Peak 1257'

Bishop's Peak 1559'

This Old House ★

San Luis Obispo

Cal Poly ★

Spirit Cycle Works

Cerro San Luis 1292'

Santa Rosa Park

FOOTHILL BLVD.

Scale of Miles

0 1 2 3 4 5

8 – MORRO BAY AND THE NINE SISTERS

RIDE AT A GLANCE

DISTANCE: 32 miles
TRAFFIC: light to heavy
BIKE LANE: in heavy traffic areas
RATING: moderate to difficult
SIDETRIP: difficult 2.1 miles

Nine volcanic peaks that march to the sea. Pristine pastures. A grove of ancient coast live oaks that once sheltered Chumash Indians and California grizzly bears. An estuary teeming with marine and bird life. A rock that has guided mariners since 1542. Add to that fresh salty air, squawking gulls and pelicans, fish and chips and a push from the wind on the way back home and you understand why this ride from San Luis Obispo to Morro Bay and back is a favorite with local bikies.

Start the ride in Santa Rosa Park in San Luis Obispo (see the SLO map at the beginning of this section). Named for Mission San Luis Obispo de Tolosa, founded in 1772 by Father Junípero Serra, life in the city of San Luis Obispo still centers around Mission Plaza and a vital downtown area. Sometime during your stay, stroll the streets of this pleasant town. For now, mount your steed and exit the park with a right turn on Santa Rosa Street (0.0) and a left turn on Foothill Boulevard (.4). Traffic on both streets is heavy, but there's a bike lane and residents are very aware of cyclists — thanks to the many self-propelled students at nearby Cal Poly.

Behind **Spirit Cycle Works** (.9) is Cerro San Luis, 1,292 feet high and the second in a chain of nine volcanic peaks that have stretched from San Luis Obispo to the sea for more than 22 million years. Born in the bowels of the earth, these peaks — composed of dacite granite — are distinctly different from the mountains surrounding them. (The first peak, 775 foot high Islay Hill, is not visible on this ride. Look for it near the SLO County Airport on rides 4 and 7.)

A bit further down and to your right is 1,559 foot high Bishop's Peak, the tallest in the chain. In the early 1900s, rock was blasted from this magnificent giant — named by the mission padres because the three points on the peak resembled a bishop's headpiece — to build the old San Luis Obispo Senior High School (since demolished), the Presbyterian Church on Marsh Street, a residence on Chorro Street and the Carnegie City Library, now the SLO County Historical Museum, adjacent to the mission. The quarry wounds are visible from Los Osos Valley Road.

At 1.3 miles, Foothill Boulevard narrows and becomes a two lane country road lined by pastures. This Old House (2.7) is a popular restaurant with locals. Built in 1919, the renovated farmhouse began serving fried chicken and beer to local cowboys in 1950. Today the specialities are steaks and ribs cooked over an oak pit barbecue.

Turn right on Los Osos Valley Road (3.4). Traffic can be heavy, but there's a wide shoulder. Next to Bishop's Peak on your right is Chumash Peak, 1,257 feet high, then 1,306 foot high Cerro Romauldo, named for the only Chumash Indian to receive a Mexican land grant in our county. In 1842, he was granted 117 acres — the smallest of the 35 grants — which he called Huerta de Romauldo (Romauldo's Kitchen Garden). Los Osos Valley Road roller-coasters through the Cañada de Los Osos y Pecho y Islay grant, a whopping 32,430 acres.

At 9.6 miles, a sign welcomes you to Los Osos, Valley of the Bears. The sign is actually a welcome from the entire South Bay community which includes the small towns of Los Osos, Baywood Park and Cuesta-By-The-Sea. Originally populated by Chumash Indians, the valley was visited by Spanish explorer Gaspar de Portolá and mission founder Father Junípero Serra in 1769. Portolá named the valley "Cañada de Los Osos", or "Valley of the Bears", because of the great number of grizzlies his party encountered.

The name has survived, but the bears weren't so fortunate. In 1772, the settlers at Mission San Carlos Borromeo de Carmelo and San Antonio de Padua faced starvation because supply ships from San Diego had been delayed. Serra remembered the grizzlies in the Los Osos Valley and dispatched a hunting party. During their three-month stay, hunters shipped 9,000 pounds of jerked and salted bear meat back to the missions. The survival of the Spanish was guaranteed, but the bear population was decimated. By 1860, the bears were no more.

But, some remnants of those earlier and wilder days remain. The Los Osos Oaks State Reserve (9.8), 90 acres of unspoiled dunes and oaks, is one of them. This land, once home to Chumash Indians, was purchased by the state in 1972. Within its boundaries are numerous coast live oaks, some over 800 years old. Walk the easy 1/2 mile trail through a dimly lit, almost eerie, world. You wind through gnarled, contorted tree trunks, ferns, mushrooms and other shade-loving plants — including poison oak! — under a canopy of intertwining, moss-covered branches. It's an easy place to miss. Just two small signs reading "State Preserve Boundary" mark the location. If you get to Sunny Oaks Mobile Home Park, you've gone too far.

Turn right on South Bay Boulevard (10.4), heading north to Morro Bay. The towering peak in the distance on the right is Hollister Peak, 1,404 feet high and the sixth in the chain. Although not the highest — Bishop's Peak has that honor — Hollister is definitely the most awesome and magnificent. Originally called Cerro Alto, it was renamed for a pioneer family who later owned the land on which it stands. Next to the giant is Cerro Cabrillo, 911 feet high.

South Bay Boulevard skirts the residential areas of the South Bay. It's well traveled, but there is a wide shoulder. At 11.7 miles you get your first look at Morro Rock and the Pacific Gas and Electric Company steam plant stacks. At 12.3 miles, the road drops down and is level with the Morro Bay estuary and its salt marshes. By 13.4 miles, the road is narrow and winding and the shoulder is non-existent.

Turn left on State Park Road (13.8). The peak that hovers on the corner is Black Hill, 665 feet high and the last of the landlocked volcanic peaks. State Park Road winds through eucalyptus, willow, pine and chaparral on its way to the bay. On the left, salt marshes reach to the mud flats and the estuary beyond. Plant and animal life are abundant here. Much of it is hidden beneath the surface of the water and in the ooze of the mud. But, as you pedal by you see great blue herons and egrets up to their knees in water and kingfishers, terns and pelicans diving for small fish.

All plant and animal life is dependent on the constant ebb and flow of the tides which bring mineral-rich water into the estuary and return life and food to the sea. Two high and two low tides occur every 24 hours. And, since as much as nine feet of water covering 2,101 acres of estuary must flow out of the narrow channel into the sea within six hours, the change is very visible. The current can run as fast as four or five miles an hour.

If you're ready for a picnic or a break, the Morro Bay State Park campground (14.6) has a wonderful picnic area. And, of course, water and restrooms are available. If you didn't pack a lunch, there's a great little cafe in the State Park Marina (14.9). Restrooms and water are also available here as are canoe rentals. If you're interested in a closer look at the life in the estuary, a paddle is definitely in order.

The area that is now occupied by the campground and golf course was once farm land. John Schneider raised hay here in the early 1900s and planted and cared for a number of eucalyptus seedlings. Those trees enhance the area to this day.

It was inevitable that developers discover Morro Bay. Miller and Murphy, a Los Angeles based firm, is responsible for building the original nine-hole golf course. There were also

53

stables, bridle paths and tennis courts. The idea, of course, was to induce inland residents to buy property and build vacation and permanent homes. In 1929, they added the Cabrillo Clubhouse, a beautiful Spanish-style building that perched on a bluff overlooking the golf links, about where the Museum of Natural History parking lot is today (15.0). The first tee was directly in front of the house and the ninth was nearby. (Today, the clubhouse — relocated to a sheltered spot near South Bay Boulevard — acts as living quarters for park employees.)

Dreams of a planned resort community faded during the Depression years. Miller and Murphy was in financial trouble and needed to dispose of its properties. In 1934, the state of California bought the golf course, White's Point (where the museum stands), Black Hill and the campground area for use as a state park. The total price was $250,000. Young men of the Civilian Conservation Corps constructed and installed the fireplaces, picnic tables, water lines and restrooms in the new state park campground. They are also responsible for the beautiful masonry drainage ditches that line the park and road to Black Hill as well as the rock portal at the north entrance to the park.

Before leaving the state park area, spend some time at the Museum of Natural History (15.0). Established in 1962, it is a cooperative effort between the California Department of Parks and Recreation and the Natural History Association, but is operated solely by volunteer docents. In addition to interpretive displays, there's a small gift shop.

Morro Bay Harbor at night.

54

After leaving the museum, continue your journey along State Park Road. The entire town of Morro Bay is a bird sanctuary. According to the Audubon Society, sightings of more than 250 different species of birds are common. The great blue heron is one of these and the best place to see them is at the Heron Rookery (15.3), a protected grove of eucalyptus between the museum and the Inn at Morro Bay. Nesting begins in January with mate selection, courtship and nest building. Eggs are hatched in late March. Then, it's pure chaos as the chicks squawk and cavort in nests 100 feet above the ground. Be sure to have binoculars and a camera ready.

Just before you leave the state park boundary, Black Hill Road (15.5) takes off to the right. If you're up to a climb and ready for a view that will knock your socks off, turn right and follow the SIDETRIP directions. If not, continue straight.

Once you leave the state park, State Park Road becomes Main Street. Follow Main to Pacific Street (16.4/18.5), turn left, then right on Embarcadero (16.6/18.7).

In 1864, Franklin Riley homesteaded 160 acres not included in either the Morro y Cayucos or San Bernardo Ranchos and, in 1870, began laying out the town of Moro. Two years later, he and a sea captain named Williams built the towns' first wharf, the beginning of the Embarcadero. The town grew quickly in the early 1870s as schooners thronged to Riley's wharf to pick up wool, produce and dairy products. But, the harbor entrance was treacherous and captains feared the high surf, surging tides and erratic winds. By the late 1800s, many ships bypassed Moro in favor of a new deep water wharf built by James Cass at nearby Cayucos.

Riley is also responsible for the profusion of eucalyptus trees in town. When he arrived, the land was covered with grease-wood and bush lupine, the only natural vegetation that would grow in the loose, sandy soil. When an area was cleared, blowing sand and rutted streets became a nuisance. So, Riley bought eucalyptus seeds, nurtured them in a greenhouse behind his home and planted hundreds of seedlings. Gradually, the rutted streets became wide avenues lined with the beautiful, sweet-smelling trees.

The Harbor Hut Restaurant (17.0/19.1) was the first eatery on the waterfront. In 1948, Evelyn Whitlock and her friend, Dolores Mesquit, turned a 14x20 military quonset hut into a cafe that served chili, clam chowder and homemade pies. That restaurant, which only seated nine diners at a time, was located across the street from its present day namesake. It soon outgrew its meager beginnings and, in 1951, Dolores and her new partner, Sara Walnum, built a brand new restaurant and motel right on the water. That building burned in 1970 and the restaurant was rebuilt as it exists today.

In the meantime, Sara married Tiger Ruse who wanted to operate a cruise boat on the bay. When he mentioned his idea to friends, they all said, "Folly"! A cruise boat in a fishing harbor was unheard of. But, Tiger ignored the sniggers and launched *Tiger's Folly I* in 1967. That boat served residents and tourists for 15 years. It was retired in 1982 and a new paddlewheeler, *Tiger's Folly II*, was launched. If time permits, take a ride on this elegantly appointed paddlewheeler, docked next to the Harbor Hut. It's a relaxing one-hour excursion in calm waters.

Construction on the Pacific Gas and Electric Company steam plant (17.1/19.2) began in 1954. Today, the three 450-foot high stacks, sunk over 60 feet in the earth, are as much a Morro Bay landmark as is the Rock. During World War II, this area served as headquarters for the naval base that was built to protect what was considered a vulnerable corner of the country. The Navy built a mock-up of a ship right next to the T-pier (directly across from the PG and E plant where the Coast Guard cutters now dock) which was used for personnel training. They also practiced amphibious landings on the beach. There was also an army artillery unit stationed in the vicinity. Its job was to guard the oil tankers and oil company properties along the water's edge between Morro Bay and Cayucos. There were gun emplacements and bunkers along the water and artillery target practice livened up the usually quiet neighborhood.

If it seems laughable that the military should have been so concerned about this quiet backwater, it wasn't. On December 23, 1941, a Japanese submarine sank the oil tanker *Montebello* off the coast of Piedras Blancas. That same night, the tanker *Larry Doheny* was fired upon in Estero Bay, near the Chevron Oil pier.

Today, Coast Guard cutters — rather than Navy vessels — ply Morro Bay waters. You can tour the two ships when they're in port. Ask at the office immediately in front of the T-pier.

Continue pedaling along Embarcadero towards the Rock. At Coleman Park (17.4/19.5), the street name changes to Coleman Drive. The park has restrooms, water and picnic facilities, all in the shadow of Morro Rock, ninth in the chain of ancient volcanic peaks. (There is a tenth sister, but it's submerged.)

Morro Rock, 576 feet high, was named by Juan Rodriquez Cabrillo during his voyage of discovery up the California coast in 1542. He called it "El Moro" or "domed turban" because of its shape. It has been a landfall for mariners ever since.

Beginning in the late 1800s, the Rock was used as a source of material for breakwaters in the state. The years of quarrying changed the shape of the monolith dramatically and, in 1968, it was declared a State Historical Landmark. Today, it's protected from all but the forces of nature. You're riding over a jetty built by the Works Progress Administration in 1933 to connect the Rock with the shore and facilitate quarrying operations. Prior to this, the rock was — according to Cabrillo — "separated from the coast by a little less than a gunshot." This jetty closed the north entrance to the harbor, but a south channel was dredged by the Army Corps of Engineers and a breakwater protecting the entrance was constructed.

Ride out to the end of the road (18.0/20.1) for a close-up look at the Rock, great views of the harbor entrance and waves pounding against the breakwater. On the harbor side, you may see a raft of sea otters that occasionally comes in close to pose for pictures. In 1973, the Rock was declared an ecological preserve, a refuge for the endangered peregrine falcon. State Fish and Game officials believe that the falcons that call Morro Rock home are one of just 50 mating pairs living in the United States (excluding Alaska).

When you've had your fill of the Rock, backtrack. Turn left on Harbor Street (19.1/21.2) and follow it through Morro Bay's business district. The **Schwinn Shop of Morro Bay** is just a half block west of Harbor on Shasta Avenue (19.5/21.6) and the city park — complete with water, restrooms, picnic facilities and a

Morro Bay Harbor from the Museum of Natural History.

57

playground — is on your right as you near Morro Bay Boulevard (19.7/21.8). Turn left on Morro Bay Boulevard then right on Quintana Road (19.8/21.9) and follow this frontage road until it meets Highway 1 (21.9/24.0) and turn right. Highway 1 is a busy, four-lane highway, but there's a wide shoulder and cycling traffic is common.

If you're up for one more bit of Morro Bay history, look to your left just past the turn onto the highway. The red-roofed adobe, set smack dab in the middle of a dairy farm, is the Canet adobe. Vincente Canet, owner of the 4,379 acre Rancho San Bernardo, hired skilled Indian labor to build his hacienda in 1841 at a cost of $40,000. The wooden floors were made of lumber brought around the Horn in sailing vessels, but the Indians crafted the other timbers from local oaks and fashioned the roof tiles from local clay. If you'd like a closer look, turn left on San Luisito Creek Road (21.2/23.3), then left again on Adobe Road. If not, keep pedaling and fly like the wind (it's at your back now) past Cuesta College, Camp San Luis Obispo, the California Men's Colony and Cal Poly State University. Can you name the peaks? They look entirely different from this side.

At Highland Drive (31.2/33.3) Highway 1 becomes Santa Rosa Street. Turn left on Oak Street (32.1/34.2) and you're back where you started — just in time for a night on the town.

SIDETRIP

The ride up to the Black Hill observation area is a bit of a challenge. But, the view from the top is out of this world. Turn right on Black Hill Road (15.5) and follow the road past the clubhouse (15.7) then veer left at the Y (15.8). You literally pedal through the golf course — watch out for flying golf balls! — through the eucalyptus planted by John Schneider in the early 1900s. It gets a bit stiff near the top, but keep spinnin' and grinnin'.

The view from the small parking area (16.5) is marvelous with the golf course, the bay, the Rock and the town of Morro Bay spread out below. But, it gets better. Lock your bike and follow the short hiking trail to the top of the mountain. You're rewarded with a 360-degree view that encompasses the hills and mountains stretching from San Luis Obispo to Morro Bay — including a birds-eye look at the volcanic peaks. To the north, Highway 1 follows the ocean to Cambria. Below is the spendor of Morro Bay. On a clear day, it's out of this world.

After you've taken it all in, turn around and coast back down to State Park Road (17.6) and rejoin the main route. The second number in the parentheses represents your total mileage.

9 — SLO CONNECTIONS
Ways to Get from San Luis Obispo
to the South County and the North Coast

Like most cities, downtown San Luis Obispo isn't much fun to cycle in. The start and stop traffic, narrow one-way streets and unfamiliar territory make sightseeing from a bicycle less than fun. So, while in town, take off your cleats, lock your bike and do what the natives do — walk.

If you're staying in town, though, you may want to ride — rather than drive — to South County and North Coast starting points. (The only way to the North County is via Highway 101, over the Cuesta Grade, to Santa Margarita. It's an option for those of you with no other transportation, but not recommended.) Or, you may just want to pedal down to the beach or do some wine tasting. Both are easily done. The following is just what the title says: a list of possible connections between San Luis Obispo and the South County or the North Coast. It's not exhaustive: for variations, check with any of the bike shops in town.

SLO — SOUTH COUNTY
From Sinsheimer Park

1. Exit the park via Southwood Drive (0.0). Continue on Southwood to Johnson Avenue (.5). and turn right. When Johnson Avenue ends at Orcutt Road (.8), turn left. A right on Biddle Ranch Road (4.6), left on Highway 227 and right on Price Canyon Road will take you to the Pismo Beach pier (about 7.5 miles) or you can connect with Ride 7 to the San Luis Obispo County Airport at the junction of Biddle Ranch Road and Highway 227. Stay on Orcutt Road to visit the Chamisal Vineyard and Winery tasting room (6.8). Or, connect with Ride 4 at Biddle Ranch Road or Tiffany Ranch Road (7.6). A right on Tiffany Ranch Road and right on Corbett Canyon Road will take you to Corbett Canyon Vineyards' tasting room (about 2.1 miles). Orcutt Road ends at Lopez Drive (9.9). Turn left and join Ride 3 to Lopez Lake (about 5.7 miles) or right to go to the Village of Arroyo Grande (about 5.0 miles).

2. Exit the park via Southwood Drive (0.0). Turn right on Laurel Lane (.3), right on Orcutt Road (.5), left on Broad Street (.9). A right turn on Tank Farm Road (1.9) and left on South Higuera Street will take you to Buckley Road where you can connect with Ride 7 returning to Pismo Beach (about 12.5 miles) or, with a little creative backtracking, Ride 6 to See Canyon (about 7.3 miles) and Avila Beach (about 9.3 miles). Stay on Broad Street (now called Highway 227) to visit the SLO

59

County Airport (2.5). A right on Price Canyon Road (5.9) takes you to the Pismo Beach pier (about 5.0 miles). A left on Corbett Canyon Road (6.3) takes you to the Corbett Canyon Vineyards tasting room (about 1.4 miles). For a climbing challenge (500 feet in one mile), follow Highway 227 into the Village of Arroyo Grande (about 6.7 miles from the Price Canyon turn-off).

From Santa Rosa Park

1. Exit the park with a right turn on Santa Rosa Street (0.0), turn left on Foothill Boulevard (.4), left on Los Osos Valley Road (2.9) and right on South Higuera Street (6.6), then follow directions in #2 above to go to See Canyon, Avila Beach or Pismo Beach.

2. Exit the park with a right turn on Santa Rosa Street (0.0), turn left on Murray Street (0.1) and left on Chorro Street (0.3). This takes you past Mission San Luis Obispo de Tolosa (1.1) and through downtown San Luis Obispo. Chorro Street ends at Broad Street (1.9). Turn left and follow the directions in #2 above to the San Luis Obispo County Airport, Avila Beach, See Canyon, Pismo Beach, Corbett Canyon Vineyards or the Village of Arroyo Grande.

The Price Anniversary House, Price Canyon Road.

SLO — NORTH COAST

The most expedient way to Morro Bay and other coastal points north is a straight shot up Highway 1 from San Luis Obispo. Start at Santa Rosa Park. It's about 11 miles to the Los Osos/Baywood Park exit (Morro Bay State Park is about 2 miles west) or 13 miles to the Morro Bay waterfront (take the MorroBay Boulevard exit). You can join the rides originating in Morro Bay or just enjoy a leisurely day then return to San Luis Obispo via Highway 1.

NORTH COAST

San Luis Obispo County

Baywood Cyclery, 2179 10th Street, Los Osos, 528-5115.

Cambria Bicycle Outfitters, 1920 Main Street, Cambria, 927-5510.

Schwinn Shop of Morro Bay, 850-B Shasta Avenue, Morro Bay, 772-2453.

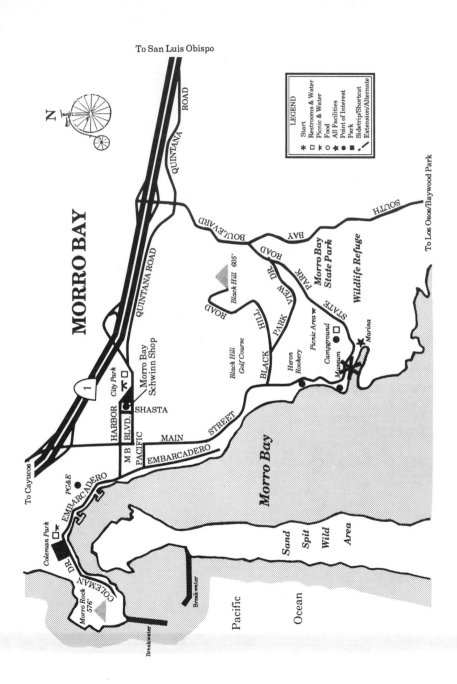

To San Luis Obispo

N

MORRO BAY

LEGEND
Start
Restrooms & Water
Picnic & Water
Food
All Facilities
Point of Interest
Park
Sidetrip/Shortcut
Extension/Alternate

QUINTANA ROAD

QUINTANA ROAD

BAY BOULEVARD

SOUTH

To Los Osos/Baywood Park

Morro Bay State Park

Wildlife Refuge

Black Hill 605'

STATE PARK DRIVE

VIEW

BLACK HILL

ROAD

Black Hill Golf Course

Morro Bay Schwinn Shop

City Park

1

SHASTA

HARBOR

M B BLVD.

PACIFIC

MAIN

STREET

EMBARCADERO

Heron Rookery

Picnic Area

Campground

Museum

Marina

To Cayucos

PG&E

EMBARCADERO

Coleman Park

COLEMAN DR.

Morro Rock 576'

Breakwater

Breakwater

Morro Bay

Sand Spit Wild Area

Pacific

Ocean

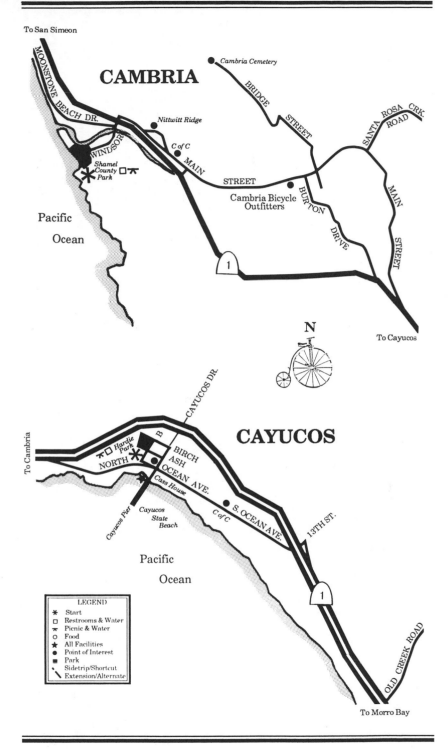

To San Simeon

CAMBRIA

Cambria Cemetery

MOONSTONE BEACH DR.

BRIDGE STREET

SANTA ROSA CRK. ROAD

Nittwitt Ridge

WINDSOR

C of C

MAIN

Shamel County Park

STREET

Cambria Bicycle Outfitters

BURTON DRIVE

MAIN STREET

Pacific

Ocean

1

N

To Cayucos

CAYUCOS

CAYUCOS DR.

To Cambria

Hardie Park

B

NORTH

BIRCH

ASH

OCEAN AVE.

Cass House

Cayucos Pier

Cayucos State Beach

C of C

S. OCEAN AVE.

13TH ST.

Pacific

Ocean

1

OLD CREEK ROAD

LEGEND
* Start
□ Restrooms & Water
⊼ Picnic & Water
○ Food
★ All Facilities
● Point of Interest
■ Park
Sidetrip/Shortcut
Extension/Alternate

To Morro Bay

63

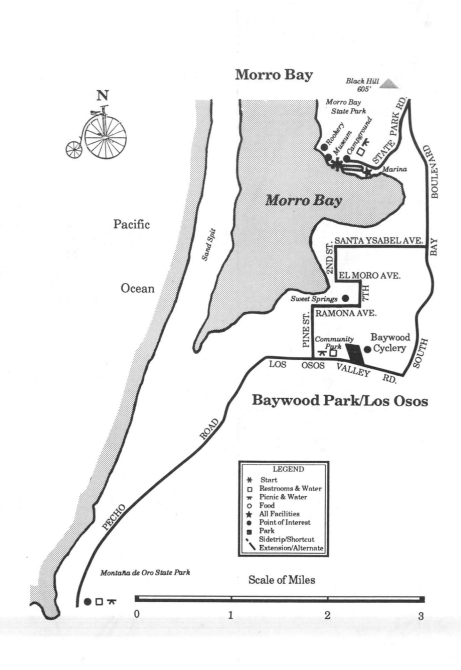

Morro Bay

Black Hill
605'

Morro Bay
State Park

N

Rookery
Museum
Campground

STATE PARK RD.

Marina

BOULEVARD

Pacific

Sand Spit

Morro Bay

SANTA YSABEL AVE.

2ND ST.

BAY

EL MORO AVE.

Ocean

7TH

Sweet Springs

RAMONA AVE.

PINE ST.

Community
Park

Baywood
Cyclery

SOUTH

LOS   OSOS   VALLEY   RD.

Baywood Park/Los Osos

ROAD

PECHO

LEGEND
✳ Start
□ Restrooms & Water
⊤ Picnic & Water
○ Food
★ All Facilities
● Point of Interest
■ Park
᠌ Sidetrip/Shortcut
＼ Extension/Alternate

Montaña de Oro State Park

Scale of Miles

●□⊤

0   1   2   3

10 — THE PECHO COAST AND MONTAÑA DE ORO

RIDE AT A GLANCE

DISTANCE:	20 miles
TRAFFIC:	light to moderate
BIKE LANE:	yes, on Los Osos Valley Road; decent shoulder in heavier traffic areas
RATING:	difficult

In 1843, Mexican Governor Micheltorena granted Rancho Pecho y Islay to Francisco Padillo. A year earlier, Governor Alvarado had granted Rancho Cañada de los Osos to Victor Linares. In 1845, these two grants — totaling 32,430 acres — were consolidated and awarded to Captain John Wilson and James Scott. Today, thanks to the foresight of the state of California, 10,000 of those acres bordering the Pecho Coast form Montaña de Oro State Park and remain as rugged and unspoiled as they were during the days of the rancheros.

In summer, fog shrouds the rugged headlands. In fall, the air is crisp and sun sparkles on the water. In winter, a raging surf pounds the jagged cliffs. In spring, the hills are carpeted with the golden heads of fiddleneck, goldfields and California poppies. No matter what the season, a ride out to Montaña de Oro is pure delight, tempered with a bit of huffing and puffing.

Start the ride at the marina in Morro Bay State Park (see the Morro Bay map at the beginning of this section). In the early 1900s, the land presently occupied by the golf course and campground was farmed by John Schneider, a Morro Bay pioneer. In addition to hay, he planted the eucalyptus trees that enhance the area to this day.

Two decades later, land developers discovered this bayside paradise. In order to attract buyers, they built the golf course and a spectacular clubhouse. But, dreams of a planned residential community faded during the Depression years. In 1934, financially troubled developers sold the golf course, White's Point (where the Museum of Natural History stands), the campground area and Black Hill to the state of California for a total of $250,000. That, of course, was the beginning of Morro Bay State Park.

Exit the marina parking lot with a right turn on State Park Road (0.0) and pedal past the golf course, campground and salt marshes and mudflats to South Bay Boulevard (1.1). The hill on your left is 665 foot high Black Hill, eighth in a chain of nine

65

volcanic peaks which have stretched from San Luis Obispo to Morro Bay for 22 million years. Directly ahead, 911 foot high Cerro Cabrillo hides in the shadow of Hollister Peak, 1,404 feet high and the most spectacular of the nine. Turn right.

South Bay Boulevard links Morro Bay with the South Bay communities of Los Osos, Baywood Park and Cuesta-By-The-Sea and, as a result, is well traveled. Initially narrow, winding and shoulderless, it hugs the tidal flats on the right and foothills on the left, offering great views of the Morro Bay estuary and the sand spit beyond.

Turn right on Santa Ysabel (2.9), following the signs to Baywood Park and Los Osos, known locally as the South Bay. In 1889, developers who hoped the Southern Pacific railroad would bypass the Cuesta Grade and route the line along the coast, laid out a town in this area and called it El Moro. Plans included residential lots and a large hotel. But, the need for an expensive bridge stopped the railroad from cutting over to the coast and El Moro languished and was forgotten.

Look for sea otters cavorting in the back bay.

In 1919, Walter Redfield, an agent selling real estate in the colony of Atascadero, came to the coast for the dedication of Atascadero Beach. During this trip he walked to El Moro and was intrigued with the possibilities. Parts of the town had been sold, but 3,000 25'x125' lots were available. Short of cash, Redfield sold 300 of the lots for $10.00 each to get enough for a down payment on a loan which would put the remaining lots in his control. Later he purchased 340 acres of eucalyptus groves and subdivided 50 or 60 acres, calling it Redfield Woods.

Redfield entertained prospects with duck hunts, fishing and strolls on the beach and, for a time, was very successful. But, the Depression put an end to his dream of a planned community with a luxury hotel and golf course. He moved to San Luis Obispo, then later returned to Baywood Park, the name given to his town because El Moro sounded too much like Morro Bay.

Santa Ysabel roller-coasters towards the back bay past a collection of cottages and luxury homes and offers great views of Morro Bay and the Rock. Turn left on 2nd Street (3.9), the main drag of Baywood Park. There are a number of shops and eateries in this area including the Omelette Shop (4.1) which is housed in the town's original post office. On Monday afternoons, a section of 2nd Street is blocked off for a farmers' market. The pier (4.2) is a local gathering place and a fun stop. There are always seagulls to feed and, if the tide is in, there are usually a few sailors launching canoes and small sailboats.

Just past the pier, 2nd Street curves to the left and becomes El Moro. Follow El Moro through residential sections to 7th Street (4.5) and turn right. Turn right again on Ramona (4.9). At the Y (5.1), stay to the left, following the signs to Montaña de Oro.

Sweet Springs, an ecological reserve, is on your right immediately after the curve. Named for the natural springs that well up and feed into ponds, this beautiful eucalyptus-shaded area was scheduled for development. But, in 1986 it was acquired by the Coastal Conservancy and, with the Morro Coast Audubon Society acting as guardian, it will remain in its natural state. There's a small parking area at 5.2 miles. From here, trails lead through the woods to the bay. In the fall, Monarch butterflies cluster in the trees. Anytime of year birds chirp and frogs croak. All in all, a very pleasant stop.

After leaving Sweet Springs, turn left on Pine (5.5) and ride the rollies through the residential community of Cuesta-By-The-Sea — developed in the 1920s — to Los Osos Valley Road (6.0). Turn right, following the signs to Montaña de Oro. When it curves to the left (6.4), Los Osos Valley Road becomes Pecho Road and begins a gentle climb. At 6.9 miles the road narrows and the climb begins in earnest, winding through eucalyptus, sand dunes and chaparral. As you duck in and out of eucalyptus, you'll get wonderful views of the ocean, the bay and Morro Rock in the distance. The climb crests at 8.0 miles. From here on you zig and zag downhill to Spooner's Cove (10.0).

The Spooner family figures prominently in Morro Bay history. Alden Bradford Spooner, a naval officer born in Maine in 1842, sailed the Great Lakes and the Pacific Ocean. Later he became a minister and came west. In 1867 he settled on Toro Creek, near the present town of Morro Bay, and became the first Protestant minister in San Luis Obispo County.

Because of his seafaring background, Spooner often piloted craft in and out of Morro Bay harbor. In 1877, the boat he was piloting capsized and he drowned. Most of his family stayed in Morro Bay, but his son, Alden Spooner II, moved to San Francisco where he trained show horses. In 1892, he returned to the Morro Bay area to farm. In 1902, he purchased 6,300 of the north acres of the Pecho y Islay grant. By 1917, he owned 8,000 acres with six miles of ocean frontage and his family lived in a simple frame dwelling on a bluff overlooking Spooner's Cove (then Buchon Landing). The old ranch house was home to Spooners — who farmed, raised dairy cattle and transported their products to San Francisco and Los Angeles via ships that moored in Spooner's Cove — for three generations. Today it is the headquarters for Montaña de Oro State Park (10.1).

In 1942, Spooner's heirs sold the Pecho Ranch. Irene Starkey McAllister who, in 1954 purchased 4,500 acres from the original buyers, renamed her land Montaña de Oro for the profusion of wildflowers that paint the landscape golden in the spring. The McAllister holding went into bankruptcy in the early 1960s and, in 1965, the state of California purchased the land for $2.6 million. Today the park occupies 10,000 acres.

Montaña de Oro remains as unspoiled as it was prior to Spooner ranching operations. The Pacific Ocean surges against 2 1/2 miles of rugged cliffs and beach areas while a scenic coastal plain extends inland to the hills. Valencia Peak, 1,345 feet high, is the most prominent geographical feature in the park. On a clear day, the view from the top extends from Point Sal in the south to Piedras Blancas in the north, a distance of nearly 100 miles.

There are over 50 miles of hiking and equestrian trails and an abundance of plant and animal life. A primitive campground, restrooms and water are available. But, there are no other services. So, if you plan on eating here, be sure to bring a picnic. There are numerous picnicking areas, including tables under the cypress trees near the old ranch house. If you see

Waves crash against the rocks at Montaña de Oro State Park.

the ranger, ask to view the collection of historic photographs housed in the park headquarters.

There's only one way in and out of Montaña de Oro so, after your visit, backtrack (the 3.0 mile round trip to the end of the road in the park and back is not included in the total mileage). Remember, what goes down must come up. The climb begins immediately and crests about 2 miles later. Then it's downhill to Los Osos Valley Road (13.8). South Bay Community Park (14.7) has restrooms, water, picnic facilities and a marvelous playground. It's also home to the Los Osos School, a one-room schoolhouse built in 1872. The school stood, for 100 years, on the south side of Los Osos Valley Road at Turri Road. It was moved to its present site in 1973 in an effort to preserve it.

If you're in need of a bicycle shop, turn left on 10th Street (15.0) for **Baywood Cyclery**. If not, continue straight and turn left on South Bay Boulevard (15.4), then left again on State Park Road (18.7) to return to the marina (19.8).

If time and energy permit, take some time to explore Morro Bay. From the State Park to the Rock, it's pure delight.

69

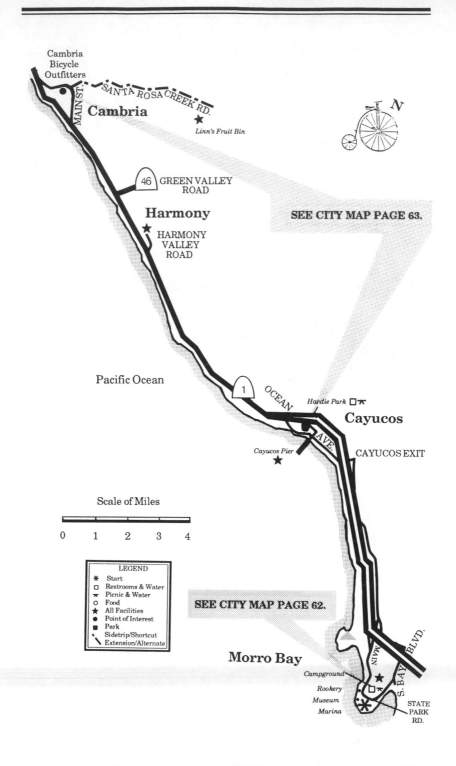

Cambria
Bicycle
Outfitters

MAIN ST.

SANTA ROSA CREEK RD.

N

Cambria

★ *Linn's Fruit Bin*

46 GREEN VALLEY
ROAD

Harmony

★ HARMONY
VALLEY
ROAD

SEE CITY MAP PAGE 63.

Pacific Ocean

1 OCEAN AVE.

Hardie Park □ 🌲

Cayucos

Cayucos Pier
★

CAYUCOS EXIT

Scale of Miles

0   1   2   3   4

LEGEND	
✱	Start
□	Restrooms & Water
🌲	Picnic & Water
○	Food
★	All Facilities
●	Point of Interest
■	Park
╲	Sidetrip/Shortcut
╲	Extension/Alternate

SEE CITY MAP PAGE 62.

Morro Bay

MAIN

S. BAY BLVD.

Campground
Rookery
Museum
Marina

★
□ 🌲
✱
STATE
PARK
RD.

11– CAYUCOS, HARMONY AND CAMBRIA

RIDE AT A GLANCE

DISTANCE:	52 miles
TRAFFIC:	moderate to heavy
BIKE LANE:	wide shoulder all along Highway 1
RATING:	moderate to difficult
SIDETRIP:	easy 10 mile roundtrip out Santa Rosa Creek Road to Linn's Fruit Bin

Highway 1, America's number one scenic highway, celebrated its 50th anniversary in 1987. Most highways are a means to an end, a route we endure for the reward at the end of the line. But California's Highway 1 is a destination in itself. Every year, motorists from all over the world include this ribbon of highway in their vacation plans. But nothing can compare to experiencing the central coast section over the handlebars.

The ride from Morro Bay to Cambria and back is a favorite with local cyclists, complete with food and rest stops in three unique villages and a push from the wind on the way home.

Start the ride at the marina in Morro Bay State Park (see the Morro Bay map at the beginning of this section). Restrooms, water and food are available here. Exit the parking lot with a right turn on State Park Road (0.0). Morro Bay State Park began in 1934 when a development scheme failed and the state was able to purchase the land. Today the park — which centers around an 18-hole golf course built originally in the 1920s — includes 1,905 acres of land and estuary. Look for great blue herons, snowy egrets and other native and migrating birds as you pedal along the bay and tidal flats. Then turn left on South Bay Boulevard (1.1) and follow it to Highway 1 (1.9) and head north.

Although the highway is a busy four-lane freeway at this point, there is a wide shoulder. If you're not comfortable riding with the traffic, take the Main Street exit (3.7) and follow the frontage road through the fringes of Morro Bay to San Jacinto Street (5.2), then get back on the highway.

In 1919, E.G. Lewis — developer of the Atascadero Colony — bought 463 acres of oceanfront land which he called Atascadero Beach. His idea was to develop a beach resort and sell property. To this end, he built a beautiful Spanish-style hotel, called the Cloisters Inn, at the foot of what is now San Jacinto Street. Lewis planted the eucalpytus trees that still line the street to enhance the avenue leading to his hotel. Many lots were sold,

71

but obtaining financing to build was difficult and only one house was erected in Lewis' time. After the financial crash of 1929, the entire Atascadero Beach property reverted to the State of California Lands Division. During World War II, the inn was occupied by officers of the 47th Regiment Coastal Artillery which guarded oil properties along the Morro Bay and Cayucos coast. When the soldiers left, the building sat empty and, piece by piece, was destroyed by vandals. Today Lewis' planned subdivision is a state beach, complete with camping facilities.

Once past San Jacinto Street, commercial and residential areas give way to rolling hills and wide, sandy beaches. The Chevron Oil Clean Seas operation (6.6) began in the 1930s. During World War II, a Japanese submarine fired on a tanker just off the end of this pier. Today you often see large tankers moored off the coast, loading or offloading crude oil.

Highway 1 is relatively flat with a few rollies to make life interesting. You can avoid one long hill by taking the Cayucos (say Ki-you´-cuss) exit (8.8). Turn left at the end of the ramp (9.0) then right on South Ocean Avenue (9.1) and pedal into one of the last great beach towns.

Once a haven to Aleut and Chumash Indians, Cayucos became a bustling commercial seaport at the turn of the century, thanks to a deep water wharf built by Captain James Cass in 1875. With easy access to shipping, European immigrants established prosperous cattle ranches and dairy farms in the surrounding area and were soon shipping beef and dairy products to San Francisco and Los Angeles.

Today the once busy seaport is a laid back resort community. But, it's a beach town with a twist. You see, Cayucos has retained its Old West charm. From the wooden boardwalks lining the front of the historic Way Station (9.9), built in 1896, to the earthy atmosphere of the Old Cayucos Tavern (10.0), to the beachfront cottages and ultramodern homes, Cayucos is a pleasant blend of past and present all rolled up into one fun-in-the-sun package.

A right turn on Cayucos Drive (10.1) takes you to Hardie Park, complete with restrooms, water, picnic facilities, a playground, swimming pool and tennis courts. Turn left to visit the site of Cass' wharf, now Cayucos Pier. As in the old days, the pier remains the center of activity in town. But today it attracts fishermen and people watchers rather than shipping moguls. At its base is a wide, sandy beach dotted with playground equipment and the occasional sun worshiper. Restrooms, water and showers are also available.

Cass, an Englishman who came to California in 1849, settled in Cayucos in 1867. He built a warehouse and a store and began work on a deep water wharf. By 1875, the wharf and his home — located directly across the street from the wharf, facing the ocean — were complete. The house stands today on the northeast corner of North Ocean Avenue and Cayucos Drive (10.1). Built with materials shipped from San Francisco, from the gold embossed wallpaper and marble fireplace to the cypress-shaded garden, it was elegant inside and out. Today the garden is overgrown with weeds and the house is in need of paint. But it stands as a reminder of the past. Some say Captain Cass never left his house. Late at night, he's been seen walking the halls, looking out to sea. Debbie Senate, a psychic and ghost hunter, says Cass is unhappy with the condition of his home. Perhaps someone will take on the restoration project and put the Captain's worries to rest.

Continue north on North Ocean Avenue and turn left on Highway 1 (10.8). At 11.1 miles the road narrows, but there is still a wide cycling shoulder. And now, the true spendor of Highway 1 begins. With rolling hills coming down to meet the road on the right and pastures rolling out to meet the sea on the left, not much has changed in this unspoiled land since the days when it was part of the 8,893 acre Rancho San Geronimo, patented to Rafael Villavicencio in 1876.

At 14.0 miles, the road starts to pull away from the ocean and work its way into the hills. It's a bit of a roller coaster, but there is no significant climbing. Don't miss the town of Harmony (18.4). It's easy to do. One long pull on a water bottle and you're past this tiny town which occupies 2.5 acres of land.

The village was originally the home of the Harmony Valley Creamery Association which produced milk, cream, butter and cheese from the early 1900s until the mid-1950s. Since then, Harmony's quiet, country atmosphere and rustic creamery buildings have attracted artists and craftspeople. Today you can watch potters, jewelers, glassblowers, woodcarvers and other artisans busy at work in their studios which also serve as retail outlets. If you're in need of facilities, there's a restaurant, ice cream shop and a saloon and, of course, water and restrooms are available. And, on summer weekends, there's live music in the shaded courtyard.

Return to Highway 1 and continue your journey north through rolling hills dotted with cows and horses, windmills, interesting rock outcroppings and old fences. The mountains on the right which frame the hills and pastures are the Santa Lucias. This range bisects the county, separating the coastal areas from the warmer inland areas. Highway 46 (20.7), also known as Green Valley Road, connects the North Coast with Paso Robles. It follows the old Cienaga Trail, used by the Indians — and later the Spanish — as a right of way over the mountains.

At 23.0 miles, turn right on Main Street and coast down this narrow road that winds through pine-covered hills to Santa Rosa Creek Road (24.2) and Cambria. *If you're going to take the SIDETRIP, turn right here and follow the SIDETRIP directions. If not, continue straight.*

In 1865, a young entrepreneur named George Lull built a general store near the intersection of the Santa Rosa Creek Trail and the coast route connecting San Luis Obispo with San Simeon, gambling that this crossroads (now Main Street and Bridge Street) was destined to boom. He was right. In 1866, the land surrounding the intersection — part of the Santa Rosa Rancho — was sold. Soon it was subdivided, streets were laid out and, within a year, a town was built. Lull's House (24.3/34.7) is still a Cambria landmark.

Originally known as Santa Rosa, Rosaville, San Simeon or Slabtown — for the rough slabs of wood used to construct the first houses and businesses — the town grew rapidly, thanks to offshore whaling and shipping, quicksilver mining, dairy farming and Chinese seaweed farmers who cultivated sea lettuce along the coastal bluffs. The name Cambria — Welsh for "Wales" — was officially adopted in 1869. It seems a Welsh businessman by the name of Llewellyn dubbed his shop "The Cambria Carpenter Shop" and the residents liked it. By 1880, Cambria was the second largest community in the county with nearly 2,000 residents living in town and on the surrounding ranches.

The Olallieberry Inn (24.5/34.9), a bed and breakfast inn, was built in the 1870s by the Manderscheid brothers, German pharmacists who owned one of the two drug stores in town during the 1880s. Two doors down is the Hilger House, built in the 1880s by the Leffingwell family. The name Leffingwell figures prominently in Cambria history. William Leffingwell, Sr. settled on the coast in 1858 and established a beach landing. Today the site of that landing is a state park day use area. He also ran a flour mill, and produced the rough slabs of local pine that went into Slabtown in his sawmill.

The Old Santa Rosa Catholic Church (24.6/35.0), built on a knoll overlooking town in 1870, was Cambria's first church. Since there was no pastor in town, the padres at Mission San Miguel traveled approximately 20 miles on foot or horseback to conduct services. Later, when Captain Cass built a Catholic Church in Cayucos, one pastor serviced both churches. Services were held in the building until 1963 when a new church was built. The abandoned church was neglected and vandalized until 1978 when community members began a restoration project. In 1982, the church and accompanying cemetery were listed on the National Register of Historic Places.

74

For a real treat, turn right on Bridge Street (24.8/35.2). Robin's Restaurant (24.9), built in the 1880s, was once home to Captain L.V. Thorndyke, keeper of the Piedras Blancas lighthouse from 1876 until 1906. Next door is the First Baptist Church. Built in 1874, the church was originally Presbyterian, but was often referred to as the Community Church since it was the only place of Protestant worship in town. It's said that President Calvin Coolidge attended a service here during a visit to the Hearst "ranch".

Once past the church, the treat begins. The road climbs through pine- and oak-shaded, undeveloped land, following the route of the old coast trail. At the end is the community cemetery (25.6/36.0), dating back to the 1870s. The Leffingwells deeded this land to the town in return for family plots. William Leffingwell, who died in 1884, is buried in a grave here marked "Gone but not forgotten." Beyond the cemetery, but no longer accessible to the public, is Phelan Grove, the site of community picnics and celebrations during Cambria's glory days.

Coast back down to Main Street (26.7/37.1) and turn right. The brick building on the northeast corner, formerly the Bank of Cambria, was built in 1930. Today this section of Cambria, known as the East Village, remains the center of business activity. Across the street, Old Camozzi's Saloon is as scruffy as it was in the 1880s when quicksilver miners came into town for a swig of whiskey and a brawl. It really rocks at night, but during the day it's relatively quiet. Go inside and read the walls. Covered with historic memorabilia, they're the closest thing Cambria has to a museum.

If you're in need of a bicycle shop, the folks at **Cambria Bicycle Outfitters** (26.9) are friendly and knowledgeable. They specialize in mountain bikes. Next door is the Bluebird Motel, built around the home that George Lull built for his bride in 1880.

The Veteran's Hall (27.6/38.0) is the official beginning of the West Village. There's a farmers' market here each Friday afternoon and next door, on the Pinedorado grounds, is the Fresnel lens used in the Piedras Blancas lighthouse from 1874 until 1949. The lens sat atop a 110 foot tower where it warned ships away from the dangerous rocks. Two years after it was replaced, it was moved to its present location. Pinedorado is Cambria's annual Labor Day celebration. Sponsored by the Lion's Club, it began in 1949 when club members wanted to raise funds for a new ambulance. Each year profits from the event benefit local causes. Also on the grounds is the Santa Rosa Schoolhouse, built in 1881, and the Cambria Jail, which housed Cambria's rowdier residents for a few months during 1917 until it was abandoned as unsafe.

Turn right on Cornwall Street (27.8/38.2) and climb a short steep hill to the Arthur Beale House (27.9/38.3), better known as Nitt Witt Ridge. Beale, also known as Captain Nitt Witt or Dr. Tinkerpaw, began work on his house in the 1920s while traveling with the Cambria Pines Developing Company. He blasted the site out of solid rock then started construction using material he salvaged, including old tires and rims (there's a bicycle wheel rim!) pipes, scraps of wood, abalone shells, ocean rocks and transluscent fence material. Beale calls his house "an historical monument to a progressive age of salvage." It takes a bit of huffing and puffing to get there, but it's worth the effort.

Return to Main Street (28.1/38.5) and turn right. You'll probably want to park your bike. The shopping, eating and browsing opportunities are almost endless. When you tire, mount your steed and ride out of town. Turn left on Windsor Avenue (28.4/38.8) then left again (south) on Highway 1 (28.5/38.9) and fly like the wind back to Morro Bay.

Leave the highway on the *second* Main Street exit (49.9/60.3) and follow Main through the business district to the state park. The entire city of Morro Bay is a bird sanctuary and, according to the Audubon Society, you may see as many as 250 different species. Perhaps the most spectacular is the great blue heron. These long legged birds stand four feet tall and have a wingspread of about six feet. The birds nest in the eucalyptus grove fronting the bay (51.8/62.2) just inside the state park boundary. Nesting begins in late January with mate selection, courtship and nest building. Eggs are hatched in late March and mom and dad take turns feeding their gangling, squawking young. By June or July the babies are fledged and by September they've left the nest completely.

If you have time and energy, visit the Museum of Natural History (52.1/62.5). Even if you're too pooped to browse, the view of the bay will knock your socks off. From there it's just a hop, skip and a jump to the marina (52.2/62.6).

SIDETRIP

Turn right on Santa Rosa Creek Road (24.2). On February 19, 1894, the Cambria Creamery began operation at this junction. The creamery had 38 subscribers, primarily dairy farmers from the Santa Rosa Creek area and south to Cayucos. It did a fair business for about 10 years, then burned to the ground. Since the dairymen had been unhappy with profits, the co-op was not rebuilt.

Santa Rosa Creek Road follows the old Santa Rosa Creek Trail which gave the ranchers — and the Indians and Spanish before them — access to the coast. In 1939, in an effort to improve roads in the county, it was oiled for the first time. Although the dairy cows have given way to beef cattle, the area remains as rural and unspoiled as it was at the turn of the century.

Pedal along the creek — past old barns, Victorian farmhouses and produce stands — to Linn's Fruit Bin (29.2). Linn's began as a "u-pick-em" berry farm. Today the roadside-stand-turned-country-store features fresh baked fruit, meat and nut pies (try the pecan!), homemade preserves, farm fresh produce and a variety of unusual handcrafted items. Best of all, the Linn's are bikies. Mr. Linn says, "We brake for bikes!" He means it, too. His sons are members of the San Luis Obispo Bike Club and the folks here knock themselves out for two-wheeled travelers. In addition to the goodies, water and restrooms are available.

Santa Rosa Creek Road continues up a very steep grade to Highway 46. But, don't go that way. *After your stop at Linn's, turn around and follow the creek to Main Street (34.6) and turn right to rejoin the main route. The second number in the parentheses represents your total mileage.*

Rustic barns dot the landscape along Santa Rosa Creek Road.

77

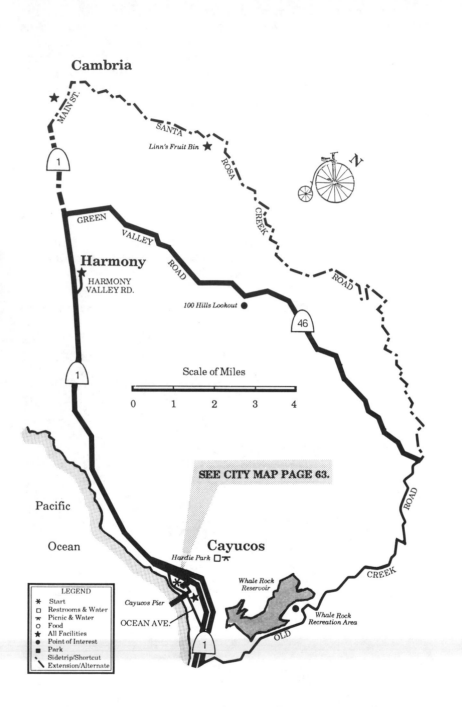

Cambria

MAIN ST.

SANTA

Linn's Fruit Bin ★

ROSA

1

CREEK

N

GREEN

VALLEY

Harmony

ROAD

HARMONY
VALLEY RD.

100 Hills Lookout ●

ROAD

46

1

Scale of Miles

0   1   2   3   4

SEE CITY MAP PAGE 63.

ROAD

Pacific

Ocean

Cayucos

Hardie Park □ ⊼

CREEK

Whale Rock
Reservoir

LEGEND
✳ Start
□ Restrooms & Water
⊼ Picnic & Water
○ Food
★ All Facilities
● Point of Interest
■ Park
Sidetrip/Shortcut
Extension/Alternate

Cayucos Pier

OCEAN AVE.

Whale Rock
Recreation Area

OLD

1

12 — OLD CREEK ROAD

RIDE AT A GLANCE

DISTANCE:	34 miles
TRAFFIC:	light to heavy
BIKE LANE:	wide shoulder on Highways 1 and 46
RATING:	very difficult
ALTERNATE:	very, very difficult 20 miles
CAUTION:	food and water and restrooms are sparse

My friend Cheryl Marek, an ultramarathon cyclist from Seattle, thinks this ride is great. She rode it in 1987 while on a training visit for the Race Across America. The best part, according to her, was when she cranked by two guys who had stopped on a steep hill and were practically dying by the side of the road. She gave them a cheery "hello" as she rode past. She will never forget the reply. In fact, she says when things got tough on RAAM, it kept her going. All the two wounded animals could manage was an incredulous, "Oh...my...God!"

Keep in mind, Cheryl didn't just do this ride. She sandwiched it in between a pedal up and down the coast — 100 plus miles. And, she did it all in about five hours.

If you're like Cheryl and enjoy stiff climbs rewarded with fantastic downhills, this ride that leaves the coast and heads east into the hills is definitely for you. Even if you don't *enjoy* climbing, you're going to love the scenery, the quiet and, especially, the downhill to the coast.

Start the ride in Hardie Park in Cayucos (see the Cayucos map at the beginning of this section). The park has restrooms, picnic facilities, water, playground equipment, tennis courts and a swimming pool. Exit the parking area (0.0) and veer to the right onto B Street. Turn left on Ash Avenue (.1) then right on Cayucos Drive (.2). Take a minute to look at the large bell in front of the fire station on this corner. Cast in 1885, it's the fire bell from the Cass warehouse.

Captain James Cass came to Cayucos in 1867. Believing that Cayucos was the ideal spot for a port, he built a warehouse and a deep water wharf, completed in 1875. Thanks to his efforts, Cayucos became a prosperous seaport. On "Butter Day", as many as 125 teams were tied to the town's 700 foot long hitching rail while dairymen and farmers arranged for their products to be shipped to San Francisco and Los Angeles via steamers docked at Cass' wharf. But, the coming of the railroad meant the end of ocean shipping. By 1915, Cayucos' heyday had ended.

Today Cayucos is a sleepy beach town, but the Cass house (.3) serves as a reminder of a more colorful past. And, the Cayucos Pier, built in the 1930s to replace Cass' storm-damaged wharf, is still the center of activity.

Turn left on North Ocean Avenue (.3) and pedal through town. The Way Station (.4), complete with a wooden boardwalk and a false western front, was built in 1876 and served as a way station for stagecoach travelers. Later, the building was used by a succession of businesses, including a bar, general store and bus station. It was left vacant and unmaintained for years following World War II but, in 1974, it was restored by new owners. Today it houses a restaurant and bar, a couple of shops and a wine tasting cellar, plus the Book Loft which overlooks the garden and outdoor dining out back.

North Ocean Avenue becomes South Ocean Avenue and, at 1.3 miles, leads directly onto Highway 1. Head south, then turn left on Old Creek Road (2.3). By 2.6 miles, you're completely out in the country, surrounded by hills and pastures.

Old Creek Road follows the Old Creek Hot Springs Trail used for centuries by Indian and Spanish travelers on their way to or from the coast. It's narrow, shoulderless and rough in spots, much like it was when horses and wagons traveled over it. But, traffic is light to non-existent. The road begins to climb almost immediately. When you reach Whale Rock Reservoir (3.9) the climbing begins in earnest.

Construction on Whale Rock Dam was completed in 1961. The reservoir, fed by Cottontail and Old Creeks, provides water for the City of San Luis Obispo, the California Men's Colony and California Polytechnic State University. The 1,350 acre reservoir and adjacent watershed is owned jointly by the State of California and the City of San Luis Obispo.

Prior to construction, archeologists studied the area and found 16 sites containing remnants of a once prosperous civilization. They reasoned that Indians favored the area because it provided protection from coastal winds and fog while giving easy access to the resources of the sea and the surrounding hills and mountains. All 16 sites were flooded by the waters impounded by the dam.

This area is rich in wildlife. In fall and winter the reservoir serves as a resting and feeding stop for Canadian snow geese as well as a wide variety of migrating ducks. Other permanent and seasonal birds commonly seen in the area include killdeer, dove, meadowlark, quail and numerous shore birds. Deer, coyotes, foxes, bobcats and the occasional mountain lion also call the area home.

Recreation at the reservoir is limited to steelhead fishing. The entrance to the recreation area is at Dead Horse Cove (5.2).

I'm sure there's a story there, but I don't know what it is. It's something to think about as you continue to climb.

The climb peaks at 5.4 miles. Enjoy the descent, but don't get too excited. By 6.2 miles, you' re climbing again, following the creek through stands of live oaks and sycamores, interspersed with avocado and citrus groves. The road twists and turns and steepens as it nears the summit then, voilà!, just when you considered getting off and walking, it crests (9.7) and you begin a marvelous rolling descent through a wide open, unspoiled landscape to Highway 46 (11.7). *If you're going to take the ALTERNATE, cross Highway 46 to Santa Rosa Creek Road and follow the Alternate directions. If not, turn left.*

This stretch of road connecting the North County across the Santa Lucia range with the coast was not completed until 1974. Prior to that, the highway ended at the junction of Santa Rosa Creek Road and travelers followed that narrow, winding path into Cambria.

Highway 46 is well traveled, but there is a wide shoulder. You climb for a bit through hills that hug the road. But, at 13.7 miles your work is finished and the Cal Trans folks want you to know it. They've posted a sign (14.3) showing a six percent downgrade for the next five miles! The view on the descent is absolutely incredible. Rows and rows of hills march to the sea. You see Hollister Peak, Cerro Cabrillo, Black Hill and, finally, Morro Rock — four of the ancient volcanic peaks that stretch from San Luis Obispo to Morro Bay. It's difficult to concentrate on the view while you're flying, so stop at one of the vista points to take it all in. Then, continue your flight through Green Valley to Highway 1 (23.3) and turn left. *If you took the ALTERNATE, this is where you rejoin the main route.*

Highway 1 is generally flat and you should have a tailwind as you pedal south through an unspoiled landscape. During the days of the Dons, this was part of the 13,184 acre Rancho Santa Rosa granted to Julian Estrada in 1841. Except for the highway, not much has changed since those days.

Harmony (25.2/45.1) is a great place to dismount and spend some time. In 1907, Morris Salmina, who was operating a small cheese factory in Cayucos, came to Harmony at the invitation of his brother Paul, a dairy farmer in the Harmony Valley. Salmina established a small cheese making plant and, because the product was so good, he immediately had support from neighboring ranchers. The Harmony Valley Creamery Association was formed in 1913 and, in 1915, it became a subscribing member to the Challenge Creamery and Butter Association, providing an assured market for all the dairy products the creamery could produce.

81

The association reached its peak of about 400 members in 1936. By the 1950s, however, membership was down to 10. Lack of permanent pastures prevented large scale dairy farming and soon dairy cows were replaced by high quality beef cattle and cheese and butter makers by ranchers.

Since then, Harmony's rustic buildings have attracted a population of artists and craftspeople. Today you can watch potters, jewelers, glassblowers, woodcarvers and other artisans busy at work in their studios. And, after all that climbing, the food, water and restrooms are Heaven indeed.

Continue your journey south on Highway 1. At 28.7/48.6 miles you emerge from the hills. Morro Rock is straight ahead and pastures meet the rugged coastline on the right. Just after the road widens to four lanes (32.6/52.5), take the Cayucos exit (32.9/52.8) and coast down North Ocean Avenue to Cayucos Drive (33.6/53.5) and turn left. Turn left again on Ash Avenue (33.7/53.6), then right on B Street (33.8/53.7) and left on Birch Avenue (33.9/53.8) to return to Hardie Park.

After relaxing on the lawn, stroll through town. It's fun and funky — definitely one of the last great beach towns.

On a clear day you can see forever from 100 Hills Lookout.

ALTERNATE

Cross Highway 46 to Santa Rosa Creek Road and prepare to climb again. This narrow, winding road follows the trail that Indians and Spaniards used for centuries to travel from the mountainous inland areas to the coast. In fact, until 1974 when Highway 46 finally bypassed it, it was part of the main route from Paso Robles to Cambria.

The first climb, which begins immediately, is steep and tough. Local bikies call it "the wall". It crests at 12.3 miles, then you begin a marvelous fast and twisting downhill through moss-covered oaks and open rangeland. When the descent bottoms out (12.6), you ride a roller coaster to the next climb (15.0). This one is equally tough. Your reward at the summit (15.6) is a tricky descent full of twists, turns and horseshoe curves and a fantastic panoramic view of hills stretching out to the sea.

During the descent, the creek plays hide and seek; sometimes it's on your left, sometimes it's on your right, sometimes it's nowhere in sight. Then, at 18.2 miles it emerges level with the road and you pedal through a magic space of water, rocky cliffs and sun-dappled pavement. There's another short climb (21.8). From your perch, the hills sweep down to the creek in the valley below. This crest (22.3) is your last. You've done your work for the day.

After one last winding descent, civilization! Linn's Fruit Bin (23.0) began as a "pick your own" olallieberry farm. Today the fruit-stand-turned-country-store sells homemade preserves and other treats along with fresh produce, handcrafted gifts and homebaked pies. Restrooms and water are also available. Best of all, the Linn's — whose two sons are members of the SLO Bicycle Club — love cyclists.

After Linn's, Santa Rosa Creek Road widens and, since Linn's is the destination of many Cambria residents and tourists, traffic is generally heavier.

This area is much the same as it was during the late 1800s when Cambria was in its heyday and dairy farms dotted the landscape. Today, dairy cows have been replaced with beef cattle, but the valley is wide open and unspoiled. By the way, you've done your work. No more climbing. Relax and enjoy your amble along Santa Rosa Creek to Cambria.

If you'd like to visit the village of Cambria — founded in 1866 to serve the whaling, mining and dairy farming industries — turn right at Main Street (28.2). If not, turn left, then left again at Highway 1 (29.3). *With the wind at your back you can almost coast to Highway 46 (31.6) where you rejoin the main route. The second number in the parentheses represents your total mileage.*

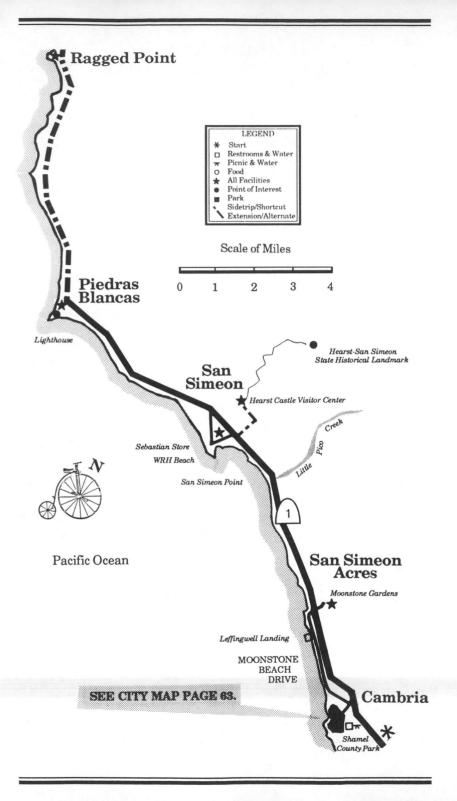

Ragged Point

LEGEND
✳ Start
☐ Restrooms & Water
⊼ Picnic & Water
○ Food
★ All Facilities
● Point of Interest
■ Park
⸱—⸱ Sidetrip/Shortcut
╲ Extension/Alternate

Scale of Miles

0   1   2   3   4

Piedras Blancas

Lighthouse

San Simeon

● *Hearst-San Simeon State Historical Landmark*

★ *Hearst Castle Visitor Center*

Little Pico Creek

Sebastian Store
WRH Beach

San Simeon Point

1

Pacific Ocean

San Simeon Acres

Moonstone Gardens ★

Leffingwell Landing

MOONSTONE BEACH DRIVE

SEE CITY MAP PAGE 63.

Cambria

✳

Shamel County Park

13 — SAN SIMEON
AND PIEDRAS BLANCAS

RIDE AT A GLANCE

DISTANCE:	30 miles
TRAFFIC:	moderate
BIKE LANE:	wide shoulder on Highway 1
RATING:	easy to moderate
EXTENSION:	difficult 15 mile roundtrip to Ragged Point
CAUTION:	Ragged Point extension is recommended only for very experienced cyclists. No shoulder on a narrow, winding road that climbs and descends dramatically. Do not attempt in summer when motorhome and trailer traffic is heavy.

"Miss Morgan, we're tired of camping out in the open at the ranch in San Simeon and I would like to build a little something ..." William Randolph Hearst wrote those words to architect Julia Morgan in 1919. The ranch he referred to, 240,000 acres strong, stretched along the coast from Harmony to Ragged Point and was comprised of the Santa Rosa, San Simeon and Piedras Blancas Ranchos. The "little something", of course, grew into his famous hilltop aerie, "La Cuesta Encantada", better known as Hearst Castle. Today, the newspaper magnate's home-away-from-home is a state monument, open to visitors. And, it is the premier tourist attraction in San Luis Obispo County.

Whether you choose to visit the castle or not, this ride along Highway 1 to the northern reaches of San Luis Obispo County is pure pleasure. You pedal past the site of a once prosperous whaling station, visit the oldest store in California, get a glimpse of the castle on the hill and see a century old lighthouse. And, if the gods are with you, you'll see zebra grazing with their fat hereford friends in pastures bordering the highway.

Start the ride in Shamel Park in Cambria (see the Cambria map at the beginning of this section). The park has restrooms, picnic facilities, water, playground equipment and a pool. Plus access to a marvelous beach.

Cambria, founded in 1865, was once known simultaneously as Santa Rosa, Rosaville and Slabtown. Today the name is certain, but the pronunciation is not. Some say "Came-bria". Some say "Camm-bria". Take your pick. Nobody makes much of a fuss about it, although locals prefer the second choice.

85

Exit the park via Windsor Avenue (0.0), then turn left on Moonstone Beach Drive (.2). Moonstone Beach, named for the smooth, milky-white moonstones that are found on the sand, is a great place for beachcombing. In addition to the moonstones, you may find agates, jade and petrified wood. And you're sure to find wonderful bits of driftwood and other flotsam and jetsam.

In 1858, William Leffingwell settled in this area and built a beach landing. Known as Leffingwell Landing (1.6), it was located at the intersection of the coast trail connecting San Luis Obispo and San Simeon Bay and the trail which came from the east, down San Simeon Creek. The beach was considered ideal for the discharge of merchandise. Timber and commodities which could be packed in barrels were floated to the landing from ships anchored off shore. Other things, including passengers, were brought ashore by rowboat. Leffingwell also established the first flour mill in the Cambria region and his sawmill produced the rough pine boards used to build the town's first homes and businesses. Today Leffingwell Landing, part of San Simeon State Beach, is a day use area with picnic and restroom facilities and wonderful views of the crashing surf.

Exit the Leffingwell Landing parking lot (mileage into the parking area *is* included in the total mileage), turn left and follow Moonstone Beach Drive until it ends at Highway 1 (2.1).

Moonstone Gardens, a three-acre arboretum and nursery, is directly across the highway. If you're a gardener, don't miss this unique nursery that's home to over 400 varieties of cacti and other succulents. In addition to the gardens, there's a cafe with patio dining and the Central Coast Wine Center, a tasting establishment representing over 50 central coast wineries. If you're not into succulents or tasting, turn left on Highway 1.

The Cambria-to-Carmel section of Highway 1 — the last link in the chain that connected Southern California with Northern California — was completed on June 27, 1937 at a cost of between $9 and $10 million dollars. Its winding course, which skirts the ocean at elevations ranging from sea level to 1000 feet, took 18 years to complete.

What we call Highway 1 was originally dubbed the Roosevelt Highway in honor of the president. In the 1950s, it was renamed the Cabrillo Highway. But, on September 21, 1966, Lady Bird Johnson and California Governor Pat Brown officially proclaimed it the nation's first Scenic Highway. You'll agree as you "oo-oo-oo" and "ah-ah-ah" past rugged cliffs, crashing surf and rolling hills to San Simeon Acres (4.4), a collection of motels and eateries spanning both sides of the highway.

After crossing Little Pico Creek (6.3), look up on the hills to your right for La Cuesta Encantada, perched 1600 feet above the

Moonstone Beach, Cambria.

sea. If you're going to tour the castle (tickets are available by calling MISTIX: 1-800-446-7275), turn right at 7.8 miles. The Visitor Information Center is just off the road. If not, turn left towards William Randolph Hearst State Beach (7.9). The park — built on land donated by the Hearst Corporation in 1951 — has restrooms, water, picnic facilities and access to the pier and beach. Continue straight to Old San Simeon (8.2).

In 1769, Gaspar de Portolá recorded his passage along this stretch of coast. Twenty-eight years later, the padres from Mission San Miguel Arcángel — situated directly 30 miles east over the mountains — cultivated this land and dubbed the area San Simeon. With the secularization of the missions, the land was divided up into three ranchos: Santa Rosa, 13,183 acres; San Simeon, 4,468 acres; and Piedra Blanca, 49,000 acres. The town of San Simeon lies within the Piedra Blanca grant.

In 1852, Captain Joseph Clark, a Portuguese whaler, bought 12 acres of land at San Simeon Point and established a whaling station. The station flourished and, at one point, 22 whalers and their families lived in the area. There were 45 buildings including homes, a general store, a blacksmith shop, a barber shop and a saloon. The general store served the whalers and the people who lived and worked on the ranchos. Since there were no roads out of this area, Clark built a wharf to serve as a landing for goods and passengers. In 1878, George Hearst replaced that wharf with a new one. And, in 1957, the County of San Luis Obispo built the pier which stands today.

The whaling station prospered until 1878. Then, since there was no employment at the site, the village gradually disappeared. The general store, however, was moved about 1/2 mile north and became part of the new town of San Simeon, owned by Senator George Hearst. Sebastian's Store (8.2) has been in continuous operation since it was built in 1852. Whalers, rancheros, fishermen and miners have done business there. And, thanks to William Randolph Hearst, politicians, movie stars and well-known personalities such as Thomas A. Edison, Calvin Coolidge and Winston Churchill have walked its floors. In 1960, the store was declared a state historical monument. Today, it continues to serve tourists and fishermen who frequent the area. In addition to groceries and gifts, there's a post office, a deli and a patio restaurant.

The other buildings in San Simeon are Hearst property. The warehouse — directly across from the store — was built in 1878. Originally, it was a storehouse for whaling, ranching and mining products shipped out of San Simeon. But, from 1919 it became the storehouse for all materials and goods used in the building of Hearst Castle. The one-room schoolhouse and homes are no longer in use. They served the needs of the Hearst family and employees during San Simeon's heyday.

W.R. Hearst died in 1951. In 1958, the Hearst Corporation gave the castle and 123 acres of gardens, terraces and palatial guest houses to the state. Today the Hearst-San Simeon State Historical Monument attracts over one million visitors annually. The house is situated on the site of the old Hearst family campground, which overlooked the 240,000 acre ranch, including 50 miles of coastline. Four castle tours are available and all include bus transportation from the Visitor Center.

Follow San Simeon-San Luis Obispo Road to Highway 1 (8.5) and turn left. Look for zebra grazing in the pastures as you pedal past the castle. Hearst maintained an extensive wild animal compound on the castle grounds. At one time, it was the largest privately owned animal collection in the world. There were water buffalo, yak, emu, ostriches, elk, eland, deer, kangaroos, zebra and llamas. The animal compound is gone, but zebra descendents remain and graze peacefully with herefords.

Highway 1 roller-coasters through rolling hills, pastures and rocky coastline. Before you know it, you're at the Piedras Blancas Lighthouse (13.9).

Piedras Blancas, Spanish for "white rocks", is the name given to this point of land by Juan Cabrillo in 1542. The twin white rocks, bleached by centuries of bird guano, remained as navigational guides — with a visibility of up to 18 miles out to sea — for the next 300 years. In 1864, during the height of the central coast whaling era, Captain Joseph Clark built a lookout at the white rocks for the purpose of sighting whales. It doubled as a lookout for ships in distress. In 1869, one unfortunate ship, the iron bark Harlech Castle, struck the largest of the rocks and was sunk. Today, that rock is called Harlech Castle in memory of the ill-fated vessel.

In 1872 the Pacific Lighthouse Board allocated $70,000 for the construction of the first lighthouse at Piedras Blancas. Construction on the brick and steel tower was begun in 1874 and completed in 1875. The original light was fitted with large glass prisms cut and polished in France. The light source was a Fresnel kerosene ardent vapor lamp with five wicks which consumed four to five tons of kerosene a year. It's said it could be seen from 25 miles out to sea. In 1949, that lens was replaced with an automatic electric beacon. The 200,000 candlepower beam sweeps across the waves twice every 15 seconds and can be seen 25 miles away. The old lamp is on display on the Pinedorado grounds in Cambria.

89

Lighthouse at Piedras Blancas.

Captain L.V. Thorndyke was placed in charge of the lighthouse in 1876 and remained there until 1906. According to legend, he left the point because he couldn't stand the noise of the new fog horn. During his 30 year stint at Piedras Blancas, Thorndyke saw the government lighthouse tender just once a year when it brought coal, kerosene and food staples. Other needed suppplies arrived every two or three months by supply boat.

The Coast Guard took over manned operation of the lighthouse in 1939 and continued in that capacity until 1974 when the light and fog horn were automated. In 1977, scientists from the National Fish and Wildlife Service moved in. They're still there, conducting extensive sea otter studies. Unfortunately, since the lighthouse in no longer manned, it's not open for tours.

The town of Piedras Blancas (15.4) has food, water and restrooms. *If you're going to take the EXTENSION to Ragged Point, continue north and follow the EXTENSION directions. If not, turn around and fly down the highway — the prevailing wind should be at your back — to Windsor Avenue (30.1/45.6), turn right and return to Shamel Park (30.4/45.9).*

If you have time and energy, a pedal or stroll through Cambria is definitely in order. Just follow Windsor Avenue into the West Village.

EXTENSION

Continue north on Highway 1. The road to Ragged Point is narrow, winding and mostly shoulderless. But, the scenery is spectacular. If you're a very experienced and confident rider, you'll probably enjoy it. If not, you definitely won't. Most of the riding is rollies but, at about 21.0 miles, you begin a steep, curving climb to Ragged Point (23.0). There's a gas station, motel and snack bar here. *When you've had your fill, backtrack to Piedras Blancas (30.9) and rejoin the main route. The second number in the parentheses represents your total mileage.*

90

NORTH COUNTY

San Luis Obispo County

Dan's Cycle and Skate, 9473 El Camino Real, Atascadero, 466-5465.

North County Schwinn Shop, 8710 El Camino Real, Atascadero, 466-2366.

Pedal Peddler, 1325 Park Street, Paso Robles, 239-2522.

Sunstorm Cyclery, 831 13th Street, Paso Robles, 238-4343.

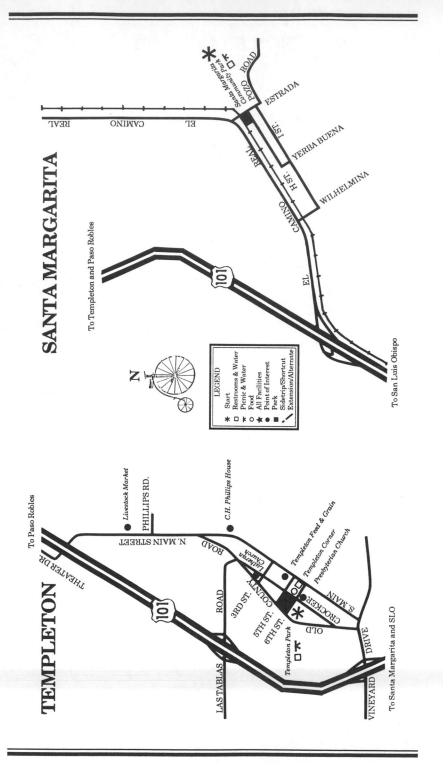

SANTA MARGARITA

To Templeton and Paso Robles

Santa Margarita Community Park

POZO ROAD

ESTRADA

1ST.

YERBA BUENA

H ST.

WILHELMINA

CAMINO

EL

REAL

EL CAMINO REAL

To San Luis Obispo

N

LEGEND
* Start
□ Restrooms & Water
⚲ Picnic & Water
○ Food
★ All Facilities
● Point of Interest
■ Park
◢ Sidetrip/Shortcut
Extension/Alternate

TEMPLETON

To Paso Robles

THEATER DR.

Livestock Market

PHILLIPS RD.

N. MAIN STREET

ROAD

C.H. Phillips House

Templeton Feed & Grain

Lutheran Church

Templeton Corner

Presbyterian Church

COUNTY ROAD

3RD ST.

5TH ST.

6TH ST.

S. MAIN

OLD

CROCKER

Templeton Park

ROAD

LAS TABLAS

VINEYARD DRIVE

To Santa Margarita and SLO

92

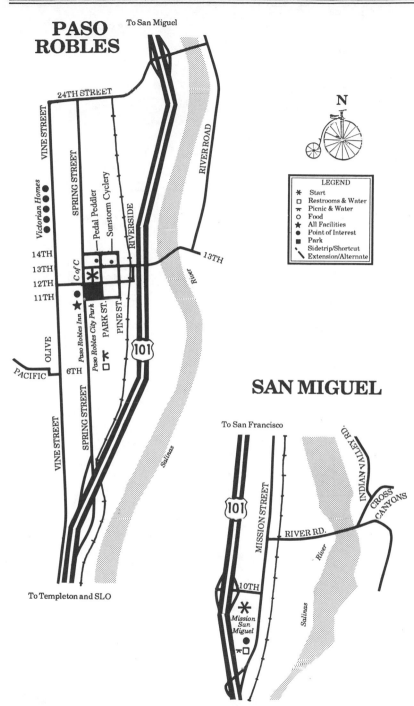

PASO ROBLES

To San Miguel

N

24TH STREET

VINE STREET

SPRING STREET

Victorian Homes

RIVER ROAD

RIVERSIDE

Pedal Peddler

Sunstorm Cyclery

14TH

13TH

12TH

11TH

13TH

C of C

River

Paso Robles Inn

PARK ST.

PINE ST.

Paso Robles City Park

101

OLIVE

PACIFIC

6TH

SPRING STREET

VINE STREET

Salinas

To Templeton and SLO

LEGEND

✳	Start
☐	Restrooms & Water
⊼	Picnic & Water
○	Food
★	All Facilities
●	Point of Interest
■	Park
╲	Sidetrip/Shortcut
╲	Extension/Alternate

SAN MIGUEL

To San Francisco

INDIAN VALLEY RD.

CROSS CANYONS

101

MISSION STREET

RIVER RD.

River

10TH

Mission San Miguel

Salinas

To Paso Robles

93

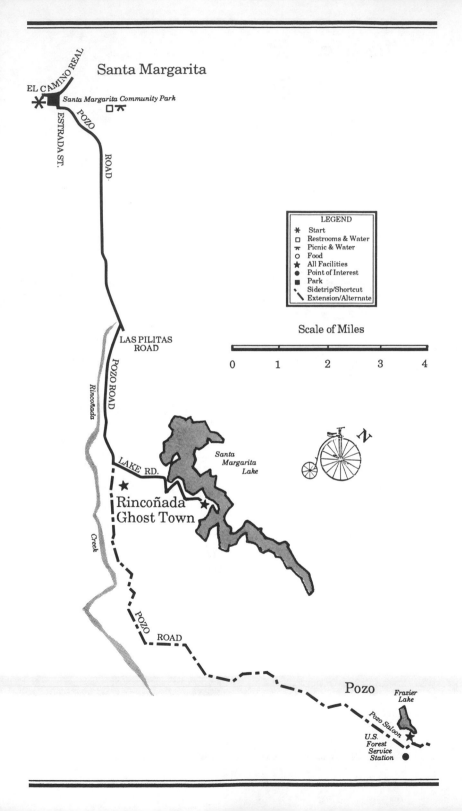

Santa Margarita

EL CAMINO REAL

ESTRADA ST.

POZO ROAD

Santa Margarita Community Park
□ ⛱

LEGEND
* Start
□ Restrooms & Water
⛱ Picnic & Water
○ Food
★ All Facilities
● Point of Interest
■ Park
╲ Sidetrip/Shortcut
━ Extension/Alternate

Scale of Miles

0   1   2   3   4

LAS PILITAS
ROAD

POZO ROAD

Rinconada

*Santa
Margarita
Lake*

N

LAKE RD.

★

Rinconada
Ghost Town

★

Creek

POZO ROAD

Pozo

*Frazier
Lake*

Pozo Saloon

★

*U.S.
Forest
Service
Station*

●

14 — SANTA MARGARITA LAKE

RIDE AT A GLANCE

DISTANCE:	18 miles
TRAFFIC:	light
BIKE LANE:	no, but very lighty traveled roads
RATING:	easy
EXTENSION:	difficult 19 mile roundtrip to Pozo Saloon
CAUTION:	the extension is recommended for experienced cyclists only

More than 200 years ago, a frail Franciscan priest, treading his way from Monterey to San Diego, paused on the steep crest of what now is Cuesta Grade. It was late August and, as he scanned the scene to the north, he saw a beautiful, fertile valley, long and flat, with an abundance of water. The land, he thought, would be ideal for raising grain and cattle to support the growing chain of young missions. The priest, Father Junípero Serra, christened the valley "Santa Margarita" — in honor of his mother — and ordered the building of an "asistencia" or assistance chapel to Mission San Luis Obispo de Tolosa.

The Santa Margarita Asistencia still stands, southeast of the sleepy town of Santa Margarita. But you'd never know it. It's enclosed in a huge barn on the Santa Margarita Ranch, successor to the 17,735 acre Rancho Santa Margarita, granted to Joaquin Estrada in 1841. Unfortunately, the building, which is a State Historical Landmark, is on private land and not accessible to casual tourists. But the valley that so impressed Father Serra is traversed by quiet, public roads, perfect for cycling.

The ride begins at Santa Margarita Community Park (see the Santa Margarita map at the beginning of this section). The park has picnic facilities, water and restrooms — well, there's a chemical toilet near the senior citizens hall, anyway. Start your odometer at the corner of Estrada and H Streets (0.0) and head east on Estrada (Highway 58). Estrada Street becomes Pozo Road (.4) and starts to climb as it leaves town. The climb crests at .7 miles, then you roller-coaster through open cattle ranges and oak-dotted hills.

Not much has changed in this country since the days of the Dons. It's open and unspoiled. At times oak trees, dripping with moss, crowd the road. At other times, hills sweep down to the road on the left then flatten out to form the banks of the Rinconãda Creek on the right. There's an occasional farmhouse, an occasional barn. And grazing cattle are king.

The Pozo Road travels through open, unspoiled country.

The Pozo Road climbs gently, tempered by rollies, out to Santa Margarita Lake Road (8.0). Turn left. Rincoñada Ghost Town is on your right. There's a general store if you need picnic supplies. Even if you don't, stop. The collection of buildings, antiques and unusual junk is worth a look.

Santa Margarita Lake Road climbs past a campground and another small market (8.6) to the lake entrance (9.1) then zips downhill to the marina. Motorists have to pay to enter the lake, but bicyclists are admitted free.

In 1942, the U.S. Army Corps of Engineers built a dam on the Salinas River to provide water for Camp San Luis Obispo. Originally dubbed the Salinas Reservoir, it was renamed in 1957 when the public was given access to the lake for fishing and

96

boating. Today, the lake — which has 22 miles of oak-studded shoreline — is, according to a ranger, "one of the county's best kept secrets." There's a marina that operates year-round, complete with bait, tackle and rental boats. And, a store and cafe that open during the summer season and on weekends and holidays year-round. Since the lake is a source of water for the city of San Luis Obispo, swimming is prohibited. But, in the summer, you can beat the heat in a swimming pool. Of course, restrooms, picnic facilities and water are available. All in all, Santa Margarita Lake is *the* place to pedal when you're looking for a quiet, relaxing day.

When you've had your fill of relaxing (mileage into the park is not included in the total mileage), head back down Santa Margarita Lake Road to Pozo Road (10.1). *If you're going to take the EXTENSION to the Pozo Saloon, turn left and follow the EXTENSION directions. If not, turn right.* After a day in the sun, the gentle downhill through Father Serra's beautiful valley to Santa Margarita Park (18.2/37.5) is most welcome.

EXTENSION

At the junction of Santa Margarita Lake Road and Pozo Road (10.1), turn left. The road narrows almost immediately and continues to roll through hills covered with oak, pine and chaparral. There are several stiff climbs on the way. The first starts at 11.8 miles and crests at 13.3 miles. The descent is steep, winding and fast on a shoulderless road with intermittent sharp drop-offs. When the descent bottoms out (15.0), you roll up and down over a series of short, steep hills until you cross the infant Salinas River (18.0). Once across, there's another twisting climb that starts at 18.2 miles and crests at 19.0 miles, followed by more short, steep rollies. The road finally levels out and, voilà!, you're in Pozo (19.7).

What's that you say? Where's the town? Well, there isn't one exactly. Unless you count the library and the Forest Service Station. Pozo — Spanish for "well" — was prosperous during the late 1800s, serving as a rest stop for travelers and a home-away-from-home for gold miners in the La Panza area and miners at the nearby Rinconada Quicksilver Mine. The saloon (19.8) began business around 1865 and closed its doors in 1920. In 1967, a former SLO County Sheriff bought the saloon and reopened for business. If you're in the area on a weekend, stop in for a cool one and a chat with the locals. It's living history.

Turn around at the saloon and backtrack to Santa Margarita Lake Road (29.5) where you rejoin the main route. The second number in the parentheses represents your total mileage.

97

Atascadero

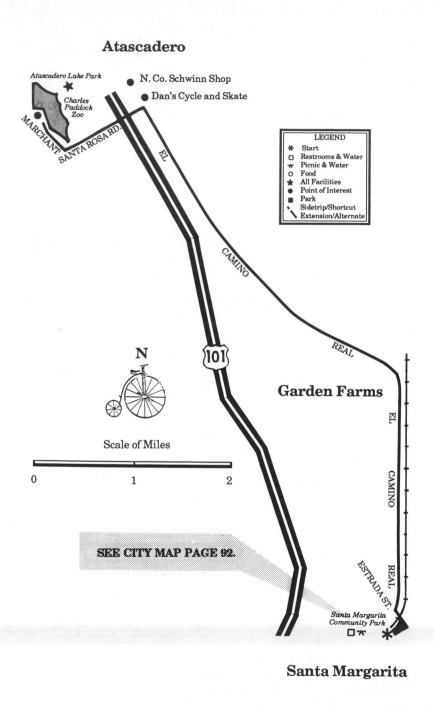

Atascadero Lake Park

Charles Paddock Zoo

MARCHANT

SANTA ROSA RD.

● N. Co. Schwinn Shop

● Dan's Cycle and Skate

EL

CAMINO

LEGEND

✳	Start
☐	Restrooms & Water
⊼	Picnic & Water
○	Food
★	All Facilities
●	Point of Interest
■	Park
⸌	Sidetrip/Shortcut
＼	Extension/Alternate

N

🛞

101

REAL

Garden Farms

EL

CAMINO

REAL

ESTRADA ST.

Scale of Miles

0   1   2

SEE CITY MAP PAGE 92.

Santa Margarita Community Park
☐ ⊼ ✳

Santa Margarita

15 — ATASCADERO LAKE PARK AND ZOO

RIDE AT A GLANCE

DISTANCE: 15 miles
TRAFFIC: light to moderate
BIKE LANE: wide shoulder on El Camino Real
RATING: easy

To paraphrase a popular saying, "The family that bicycles together, stays together." Sometimes that means a challenging century or an extended tour. More often than not, it means an easy pedal to a pleasant destination. If your family's in the mood for a laid back outing, complete with a picnic, an after-lunch ball game, a nap in the shade and a boat ride — not to mention a visit with bears and tigers and jaguars, oh my! — this ride from Santa Margarita to the southern fringes of Atascadero is definitely for you. It's a great way to spend a warm, lazy day.

Start the ride at Santa Margarita Community Park (see the Santa Margarita map at the beginning of this section). The park has water, picnic facilities, a playground and, if you call a chemical toilet a restroom, it has that, too. Exit the park via Estrada Street, go west to El Camino Real (0.0) and turn right.

Before U.S. 101 bypassed Santa Margarita, El Camino Real was a well-traveled road. Today it's used primarily by locals commuting between Santa Margarita and Atascadero. There's no marked shoulder, but the road is wide and cycling is safe.

The ride out El Camino Real is not especially exciting or scenic, but it's pleasant. You roll along, following the Southern Pacific Railroad tracks, through a semi-rural landscape. Horses and cattle dot the foothills, bordered by the freeway to the west and the Santa Lucia Range to the east. If you're into antiques and collectibles, Wagon Wheel Antiques in Garden Farms (1.7) makes a fun stop. As you near Atascadero, big ranches give way to small acreages dotted with large, modern homes. Near Atascadero State Hospital (5.7), condominiums, apartments and mobile home parks take over.

If you're in need of a bike shop, **Dan's Cycle and Skate** is in the shopping center on your right just past Santa Rosa Road (6.3) and **North County Schwinn Shop** is just .5 miles down El Camino Real on your left. If not, turn left on Santa Rosa Road and follow it across the freeway (6.4), then coast downhill — through oak-studded residential areas — to Marchant Way (7.3) and Atascadero Lake. Turn right and follow Marchant Way along the curving lakeshore to the park entrance (7.7).

99

The city of Atascadero was a dream-come-true for Edward Gardner Lewis, an eastern businessman who bought the 23,000 acre Atascadero Rancho in 1913. His goal was to establish a self-sufficient community — one whose buildings, bridges, streets, water systems and recreational facilities were planned by master architects and executed by competent contractors.

Prior to Lewis' involvement, Congress had considered building a permanent military training facility on the rancho. Water, of course, was a big concern and the natural reservoirs fed by Atascadero Creek and several smaller streams appealed to the officers researching the site. Their idea was to provide water to the valley — and the soldiers training there — through a network of pipes originating at the reservoirs.

Fortunately for us, the Army opted for a site north of Atascadero on the Nacimiento Ranch. When Lewis bought the land, he, too, realized the importance of the natural reservoirs. But, his plan was for recreational, not practical, use. He had his engineers construct a dam across the low end of the largest reservoir and scoop out the mud in the valley below. The result was Atascadero Lake, referred to by early colonists as "Lewis' gem".

In 1924, Lewis lost financial backing and went bankrupt, his dream incomplete. But, many of his successes — including the lake and the park surrounding it — remained as monuments to his endeavors.   In 1934, the County of San Luis Obispo bought the lake property and, in 1939 — thanks to a WPA project — it was enlarged and improved. It became city property in 1979 when Atascadero was incorporated.

There's lots to do at the park. If you want to keep your legs limber, head for Pop's Tackle Shop and take a spin across the lake in a pedal boat. If you'd rather relax, Pop's rents fishing tackle, too. There's playground equipment, picnic tables, restrooms and water plus ducks to feed, grass to run in and trees to snooze under. And, a real treat for the whole family — a zoo.

Charles Paddock, Superintendent of Atascadero Lake Park, started the zoo in 1955 with a pet possum and a love of exotic animals. When his hobby outgrew his backyard and living room, he moved an abandoned dog kennel and his burgeoning animal collection to the lake.   Later he built bigger enclosures and landscaped the grounds. Today the city provides full support for the zoo, aided by the San Luis Obispo County Zoological Society. The nicely landscaped, three-acre site is home to pair of Bengal tigers, a cougar, two jaguars, monkeys, flamingoes, alligators and more.   And, there's a wonderful petting zoo. The zoo is open 10:00 a.m. to 4:00 p.m. daily. Admission is free, but nominal donations are appreciated.

A fine-feathered flamingo, Charles Paddock Zoo.

After your day in the park, pack up the kids and your picnic gear, mount your steeds and backtrack on Marchant Way to Santa Rosa Road (8.0). Turn left and follow Santa Rosa Road to El Camino Real (9.1). Turn right and ride the rollies back to Estrada Street (15.4) and Santa Margarita Community Park.

In 1884, thanks to the building of the Southern Pacific Railroad, Santa Margarita was the largest town between San Jose and Santa Barbara. Some 4,000 workers were housed here during the six years it took to extend the line to San Luis Obispo, 13 miles and six tunnels south. But, the heyday ended in 1890 when work was completed and the tracks pushed south. If you have time and energy, stroll through town. There's a mercantile, liquor store, hardware store, post office, auction barn and a few antique shops — all reminiscent of the days when the iron horse made Santa Margarita queen, if just for a day.

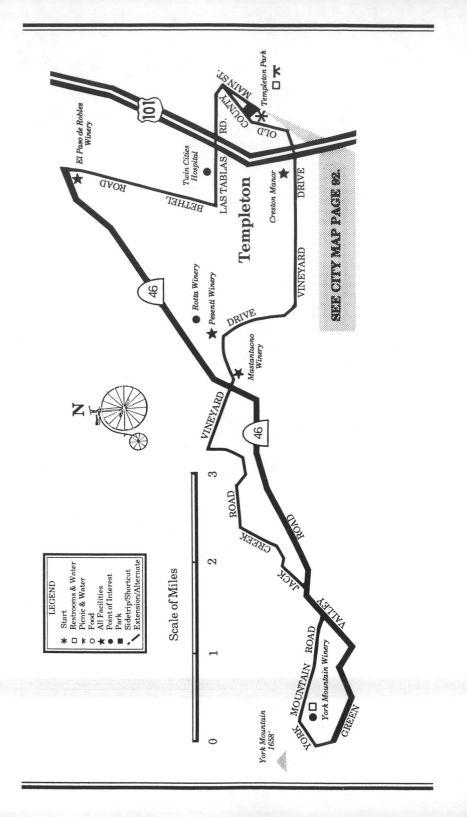

16 — NORTH COUNTY WINE COUNTRY

RIDE AT A GLANCE

DISTANCE:	20 miles
TRAFFIC:	light to moderate
BIKE LANE:	wide shoulder on Highway 46
RATING:	moderate to difficult

The northern section of San Luis Obispo County is wine country. Vineyards line the hills from San Miguel in the north to Templeton in the south, supplying grapes for 20 plus commercial wineries. But, until just a few years ago, there were only three wineries in the county. They clustered like grapes in the hills west of Templeton. Today, several newer wineries have joined the cluster and this leisurely spin through rolling hills and snug valleys takes them all in.

Start the ride in Templeton Park (see the Templeton map at the beginning of this section). Templeton, founded in 1886, is the brain child of Chauncey H. Phillips, a land promoter who persuaded Southern Pacific Railroad executives to run tracks from Paso Robles, through his property, to the site of his new town.

Templeton — named in honor of Templeton Crocker, son of Southern Pacific's vice president — prospered until 1889 when the line pushed through to Santa Margarita on its way south to San Luis Obispo and Santa Barbara.

Today, Templeton, off the beaten track of Highway 101, is a quiet town with western charm. Take time to explore Main Street. In fact, you might want to start your wine tasting at Templeton Corner (on the corner of 6th and Main Streets). This wine tasting establishment represents many small, family-run wineries in San Luis Obispo County, offering you the opportunity to sample the nectar of smaller wineries that don't have tasting rooms. It also has a great deli.

Start your odometer on the corner of 6th and Crocker Streets (0.0). The Presbyterian church on the corner was built in 1887 and continues to serve the religious needs of Templeton's Presbyterian residents. It was built with redwood lumber shipped to Cass' wharf in Cayucos then hauled by wagon over York Mountain. In fact, all of Templeton's original buildings — excluding the Bethel Lutheran Church — were made of wood. In 1897, a fire swept through Main Street, destroying most of the commercial structures. Undaunted, Templeton's business community rebuilt the town. But, this time contractors used locally made adobe brick.

Turn left on Old County Road (.1) then right on Vineyard Drive (.5). Creston Manor's tasting toom (.8) is your first stop. This is one of the new kids on the block. Actually, the winery is not on the block at all, but many miles — and several hard climbs — southeast of here on Highway 58 near La Panza Road. But, you can taste their wines at this tree-shaded spot, complete with picnic tables, clean restrooms and water. There's also a nice selection of cheese, breads, olives and pickles if you're in need of picnic fixin's.

After leaving Creston Manor (the mileage into the tasting room is not included in the total mileage), continue west on Vineyard Drive, riding the rollies of this lightly-traveled road through small acreages dotted with large homes.There's a short climb up to Pesenti Winery (3.3), one of the three grapes on the original cluster. Founded in 1934 by Frank Pesenti, it's still family operated. Tours are available and the tasting room has food, soft drinks and gifts plus restrooms and water.

Pesenti's neighbor, Rotta Winery, was built in 1856, making it the oldest winery in the area. Unfortunately, the winery is now closed, but the beautiful old world building still stands on Winery Road, just behind Pesenti.

Continue to pedal west on Vineyard Drive (the mileage into Pesenti is not included in the total mileage). You climb — just a bit — through hills covered with Pesenti vines and ancient oaks, then zip downhill to Mastantuono Winery (3.9). Although most of Mastantuono's winemaking is done at its Willow Creek facility — a few miles northwest of here — there is a small winery and barrel storage below the tasting room built in 1983. In addition to tasting, Mastantuono offers picnic facilities, picnic supplies, restrooms, water and a great collection of antique wine-related paraphernalia.

Turn left on Highway 46 (4.0). This road, which connects the North County with the coast, is fairly well traveled. But, there is a wide shoulder. You roll up and down through moss-clad oaks and pastures and farmland framed by rolling hills. At 6.2 miles you start a good, stiff climb. Don't get too excited at the crest (8.0). Just after the right turn on the *second* York Mountain Road (8.2), you climb some more. This time on a narrow, twisting road strewn with eucalyptus seed pods and oak leaves. The work's over at 8.6 miles and you coast — twisting and turning all the time — to York Mountain Winery (8.8).

York Mountain Winery, established in 1882 by Andrew York, is the oldest continuously operating winery in San Luis Obispo, Santa Barbara and Monterey Counties. The beautiful brick building houses a comfortable tasting room and a display of antique machinery and memorabilia and 100-year-old casks. In addition to its age, York Mountain Winery has another claim to fame. During the early 1900s when Ignace Jan Paderewski called Paso Robles home (see Ride 7 — Peachy Canyon Road), the Polish pianist and statesman commissioned York Mountain Winery to produce his San Ignacio Zinfandel, made from grapes grown on his 2,500 acre ranch. The wine was a gold medal winner, known throughout the world for its quality.

When you leave the winery, turn right, continuing east on York Mountain Road. The ride down is winding, fast and fun. You twist and turn, shaded by oaks festooned with moss and mistletoe, to Highway 46 (10.4). Turn left, continue to coast to Jack Creek Road (11.1) and turn left again. Jack Creek Road is narrow and a bit rough at times, but it's pure cycling pleasure. For me, the quiet journey through oaks, hills and pastures ends too soon. Turn right on Vineyard Drive (12.9), roll up and down to Highway 46 (13.6) and turn left. There's a bit of a climb after the turn, but it crests at 14.5 miles. Then you zip downhill, right through the hills, to Bethel Road (16.7).

Turn right on Bethel Road, shift down, stand on the pedals, and climb up a short, steep hill to the entrance to El Paso de Robles Winery (16.9). Established in 1981, this is one of the Templeton area's newer wineries. The Spanish style building sits amid 11 acres of vineyards. There's a cozy tasting room, complete with gifts and food, and an outdoor patio, perfect for a picnic. Of course, restrooms and water are also available.

When you leave El Paso de Robles Winery (the mileage into the tasting room is not included in the total mileage), turn right on Bethel Road. The vineyards to your left belong to Fairview Farm, another of the new kids on the block. Tasting here is by appointment only, but you get a wonderful view of the prosperous vineyards — planted in 1972 — from the road. Follow Bethel Road — there are a lot of short, steep "ups" and wonderful "downs"—to Las Tablas Road (18.6) and turn left.

Las Tablas Road passes Twin Cities Community Hospital (19.0), rolls up and down to the freeway (19.4), then twists, turns and descends to Old County Road (20.0). Turn right, then stay to the right at the fork, taking Old County Road past the Bethel Lutheran Church (20.1), built by Templeton's Swedish community in 1887. Turn left on 6th Street (20.3) to return to Templeton Community Park and your starting point (20.4).

I don't know about you, but I'm glad Templeton didn't boom like Phillips had hoped. I enjoy the peace and quiet. And, after my "grape" expedition, I especially enjoy lying in the shade in the park he so graciously donated to the town of his dreams.

105

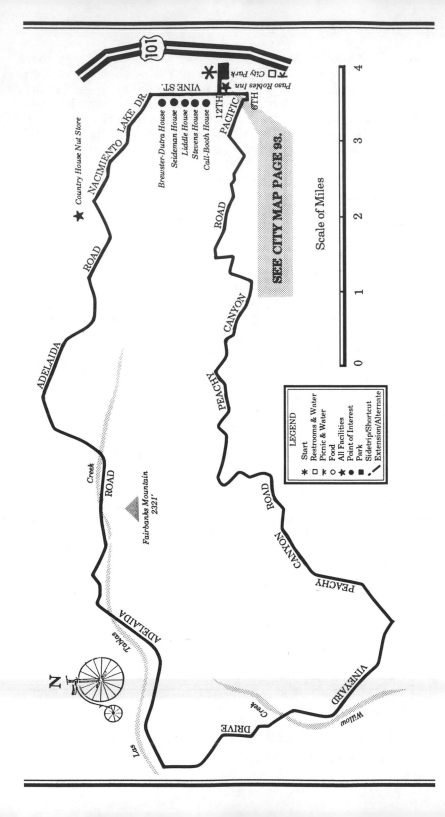

101

City Park
Paso Robles Inn
VINE ST.
12TH
PACIFIC
6TH

Brewster-Dufra House
Seideman House
Liddle House
Stevens House
Call-Booth House

NACIMIENTO LAKE DR.

Country House Nut Store

ROAD

ADELAIDA

Creek

ROAD

Fairbanks Mountain
2321'

ROAD

CANYON

PEACHY

SEE CITY MAP PAGE 93.

Scale of Miles

0   1   2   3   4

LEGEND
Start   *
Restrooms & Water   □
Picnic & Water   ⊤
Food   ○
All Facilities   ★
Point of Interest   ●
Park   ■
Sidetrip/Shortcut   ⌐
Extension/Alternate   .⌐

ROAD

CANYON

PEACHY

VINEYARD

Willow

ADELAIDA

Las Tablas

Creek

DRIVE

N

17 — PEACHY CANYON ROAD

RIDE AT A GLANCE

DISTANCE:	28 miles
TRAFFIC:	light to moderate
BIKE LANE:	yes, on Vine Street in Paso Robles; wide shoulder on Nacimiento Lake Drive
RATING:	difficult

When I was preparing to write this book, I asked local bikies what rides they thought should be included. Jim Delany, a South County resident and faculty advisor for the Cal Poly Wheelmen, suggested this one. He says he'd drive up to Paso Robles any day just to ride out Peachy Canyon Road and back. I have to admit, I didn't know the road. But, once I discovered it, it slipped very nicely into my cycling repertoire. It's one of those rides you do just for the pure pleasure of it. There's little or no traffic most of the way and the terrain is gently rolling — with just enough climbing to make pedaling interesting. Add to that some wonderful downhills with good twists and turns and you'll understand why Jim recommended this spin through an unspoiled landscape dotted with oaks, vineyards and almond orchards.

Start the ride at Paso Robles City Park (see the Paso Robles map at the beginning of this section).Water, restrooms, playground equipment and picnic facilities are available here as is the city library, built in 1907 with funds donated by Andrew Carnegie.

Unlike its neighbors to the north and south, Paso Robles was a popular stop on the stage route long before the railroad came through in 1886. In fact, travelers went out of their way to visit the bubbling hot springs and therapeutic mud baths at El Paso de Robles Hotel and Hot Springs, a privately owned village established in 1857 and built around the natural hot springs once enjoyed by Indians, grizzly bears and mission padres.

In 1914, Ignace Jan Paderewski, the Polish pianist and statesman, was stricken with neuritis while giving a concert in Seattle. He rushed to San Francisco for medical treatment, but a friend urged him to forget about doctors and go to Paso Robles and take the mud baths. Paderewski and his retinue moved into a suite of rooms at El Paso de Robles Hotel in January, 1914. The mud baths, hot sulphur baths and therapeutic massage seemed to do the trick for Paderewski's malady and he stayed at the hotel for the next eight years, then continued to return to the inn and his ranch west of town until his death in 1941.

El Paso de Robles Hotel and Hot Springs burned to the ground in June, 1941. Six months later, Paderewski died. The new hotel — the Paso Robles Inn, located on Spring Street just across from the park — is built with the charred bricks of the hotel Paderewski loved.

Head west on 12th Street and start your odometer at the northwest corner of the park, 12th and Spring Streets (0.0). Cross Spring Street, then turn left on Vine Street (.1) and follow it through a pleasant mixture of Victorian and newer homes to 6th Street (.6). Turn right on 6th, jog right on Olive Drive (.7), then immediately jog left on Pacific Avenue. When Pacific Avenue becomes Peachy Canyon Road (1.3), you're out in the country, cycling through hills dotted with orchards, oak-filled canyons, and rugged, wide open country. The terrain is rolling with a few good climbs. It's quiet, peaceful country.

Orchards give way to vineyards at Hidden Mountain Ranch (6.8), a grape-growing operation tucked in the foothills of the Santa Lucia Range. The sun-dappled road, canopied by giant oaks dripping with moss, is rough and narrow and continues to climb and descend through country that is outrageously beautiful — a mixture of vineyards, orchards and natural, oak-studded terrain. At 8.1 miles, you've done most of the work. Now the road twists, turns and descends to Vineyard Drive (11.6) where you turn right.

Vineyard Drive descends gently, at first, through rolling hills covered with vineyards (what else!). Then it rolls along, following Willow Creek, through oak-covered hills punctuated with farmhouses and ranch land. Turn right at Adelaida Road (15.8), then climb gently through open rangeland to acres and acres of almond orchards (19.1). In spring (usually mid-February through early March), the pink blossoms are gorgeous, their perfume wonderful. The climb peaks at Hilltop Ranch (19.7), then you descend through more oaks, more orchards, more rolling hills to Nacimiento Lake Drive (25.0) and turn right. If you'd like a taste of organically grown Paso Robles almonds, stop in at the Country Nut House Store on the Jardine Ranch (25.1). Then follow busy Nacimiento Lake Drive to Vine Street (26.7) and turn right.

Vine Street rolls through Paso Robles' original residential district. There are several Victorians of note, all on your right hand side: the Bonde House (27.0), built circa 1890; the Brewster-Dutra Home (27.1), built in 1803 and now on the National Register of Historic Places; the Seideman House (27.4), built in 1892, now home to Roselith, a bed and breakfast inn; the Liddle House (27.5), built in 1889; and, right next door, the Stevens House, built in 1892. Last, but certainly not least, the Stevens

Springtime, Peachy Canyon Road and Vineyard Drive.

House neighbor, the Call-Booth House (27.6), built in 1893. This Queen Anne style cottage — originally the home of Dr. Samuel Johnson Call, resident physician at El Paso de Robles Hot Springs — now houses the Paso Robles Art Association Gallery. As you stroll through the house with its original fixtures and antique furnishings and the formal Victorian garden, you get a taste of what life was like in turn-of-the-century Paso Robles.

Turn left on 12th Street (27.6) and cross Spring Street (27.8) to return to Paso Robles City Park (27.9).

If you thought Paderewski was Paso Robles' only famous resident, think again. Legend has it that Frank and Jesse James spent time with their Uncle Drury James — part owner of the El Paso de Robles Hotel and Hot Springs — in between their notorious feats of derring-do in 1869 and 1870. It seems the boys — on their good behavior while here — enjoyed their stay in San Luis Obispo County and, when the time came to move on, they were reluctant to go. Perhaps they didn't. Some say their ghosts haunt Drury James' old La Panza Ranch to this day. Whether fact or fiction, it's fun to think about, relaxing in the shade in the park James and his partner, Blackburn, donated to the city in 1897.

109

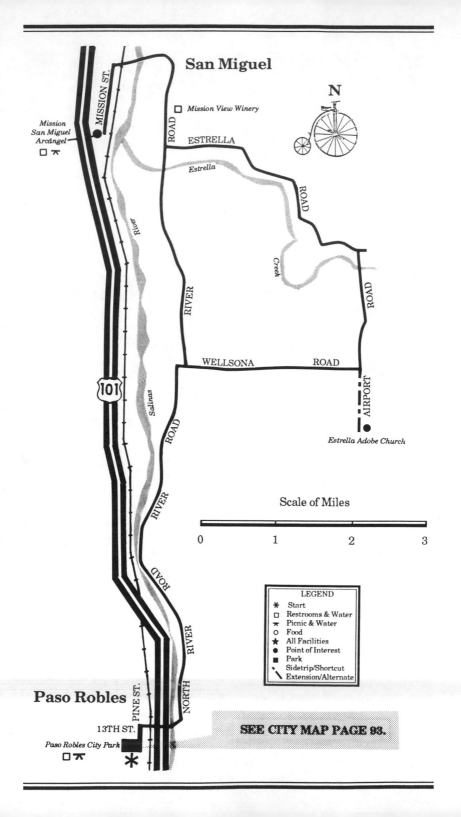

San Miguel

N

□ Mission View Winery

Mission
San Miguel
Arcángel
□ ⊼

MISSION ST.

ROAD

ESTRELLA

Estrella

ROAD

River

Creek

RIVER

ROAD

WELLSONA   ROAD

101

Salinas

ROAD

AIRPORT

Estrella Adobe Church

RIVER

Scale of Miles

0   1   2   3

ROAD

RIVER

NORTH

Paso Robles

PINE ST.

13TH ST.

Paso Robles City Park
□ ⊼   ✳

SEE CITY MAP PAGE 93.

LEGEND
✳ Start
□ Restrooms & Water
⊼ Picnic & Water
○ Food
★ All Facilities
● Point of Interest
■ Park
╲ Sidetrip/Shortcut
╲ Extension/Alternate

18 — MISSION SAN MIGUEL ARCÁNGEL

RIDE AT A GLANCE

DISTANCE:	29 miles
TRAFFIC:	light to moderate
BIKE LANE:	no
RATING:	easy to moderate
SIDETRIP:	easy 2.2 mile round trip to Estrella Adobe

Northern San Luis Obispo County is ranch country. I love to pedal past the old farmhouses, rustic barns and the new, modern ranch homes, marveling at the lifestyle and wondering about the fanciful names chosen to adorn signposts and brand cattle. There's Star Farms and Paso Miguel. Skyline Station and Rancho Flores. Los Robles Ranch and the Slash C. Then, there's my favorite: Almost A Ranch. See if you can spot it on this pleasant ride from Paso Robles to Mission San Miguel Arcángel and the Estrella plains.

Start the ride at Paso Robles City Park (see the Paso Robles map at the beginning of this section). James and Daniel Blackburn and Lazarus Godchaux bought the 25,993 acre El Paso de Robles Rancho from Petronillo Rios in 1857. At that time, the only building existing on the land the city now occupies was no building at all, but the remains of a log shack.

The shack surrounded a bubbling hot spring and was built in the early 1800s by a father from Mission San Miguel Arcángel. The Franciscans had long been aware of the healing powers of the hot sulphur water and made pilgrimages to El Paso de Robles from as far away as Santa Inéz and San Luis Obispo.

The Blackburn brothers knew a good thing when they saw it. By the early 1860s, they had replaced the shack with a prosperous stagecoach-era resort and health center. By the time the railroad came through in 1886, the town of Paso Robles had been surveyed and lots had been laid out.

In 1897, Daniel Blackburn and Drury James — his new partner — donated two full city blocks in the heart of town to be used as a public park. That's where you are now. After the park was laid out, town residents had a planting day and prominent citizens donated a tree or shrub. For years, the new plantings were referred to by the donor's name. Today there's a guide near the center of the park that points out the early plantings. The park has picnic facilities, a playground, water, restrooms and ... a library. The stone building dominating the park was built in 1907 with funds donated to the city by Andrew Carnegie.

111

Start your odometer on the corner of 12th and Pine Streets (0.0) and head east on 12th. Turn left on Riverside Avenue (.1) then right on 13th Street (.2). Follow 13th across the Salinas River (.3) then turn left on North River Road (.4). At the Y (.5) stay to the left, following the river.

North River Road is narrow and, at times, rough. But, there is little or no traffic. You pedal along the usually dry Salinas River through rolling hills sprinkled with cattle, horses, white fences and the occasional farmhouse and barn. It's relatively flat with a few rollies to make the pedaling interesting.

Rolling Ridge Winery (8.7), established in 1983, is not open for tasting. (You can sample its wines at Templeton Corner.) But, Mission View Winery (9.5) is. If you're in the mood, turn right off of North River Road and follow the driveway to the winery. Tours and tasting here are far from routine and often include a trip into the vineyard. After Mission View (mileage into the winery is not included in the total mileage), continue north on River Road, cross the Salinas River (9.9), turn left on Mission Street (10.4) and follow it through the town of San Miguel to Mission San Miguel Arcángel (11.0).

Mission San Miguel Arcángel was founded in 1797 by Father Fermín Francisco de Lasuén, Father Serra's successor. It was number 16 in the chain of 21 and bridged the gap between Mission San Antonio de Padua and Mission San Luis Obispo de Tolosa. Because of its location on the Salinas River, mission workers were able to grow vast amounts of grain and raise large herds of cattle. After secularization in 1836, the mission was subjected to a number of indignities including use as a barn, saloon, dance hall and living quarters. In 1848, it was the scene of the grizzly murder of 11 people living on the premises. Those people are buried in the cemetery adjoing the mission and it's said their ghosts haunt the mission rooms.

Mission San Miguel was returned to the Franciscan friars in 1929. They began immediate restoration in an effort to keep the structure as authentic as possible. Many of the original decorations — including the frescoes painted by Estéban Munras in 1823 — are still intact and the church is considered to have the best preserved interior of any of the California missions.

San Miguel is one of four missions still attended by brown-robed Franciscan friars. Strolling the grounds, they add a touch of history often lacking at some of the glitzier missions.

After visiting the mission, backtrack on Mission Street to River Road (11.6) and turn right. Then backtrack again to Estrella Road (13.5) and turn left.

The terrain on Estrella Road alternates between flat and rolling. You meander past hills covered with vineyards and

112

prosperous farms and ranches, then turn right on Airport Road (16.9), dip through Estrella Creek (17.0) and roll up and down to Wellsona Road (18.5). *If you're going to take the SIDETRIP, continue straight on Airport Road and follow the SIDETRIP instructions. If not, turn right on Wellsona Road.*

Wellsona Road is a bit rough, but it is paved and there's very little traffic. You'll enjoy the gentle downhill through vine-yards, rolling pastures and, finally, large homes dotting pros-perous ranches to the junction of River Road (23.0/25.2). Con-tinue straight and follow River Road back to Paso Robles. Turn right on 13th Street (28.2/30.4), left on Riverside Avenue (28.4/30.6) and right on 12th Street (28.5/30.7) to return to Paso Robles City Park (28.6/30.8).

Before you pack it all in, pop over and see the folks at **Pedal Peddler**, on Park Street between 13th and 14th Streets, and **Sunstorm Cyclery**, on 13th Street between Park and Pine Streets. Then, head for Licketysplit (across the street from Sunstorm), the local purveyor of Burnardo'z ice cream for a post ride treat.

SIDETRIP

Stay on Airport Road and pedal across the Estrella plains. For years, pioneers in the county assumed this land east of Mission San Miguel was part of a Mexican land grant. But, that assumption proved false.

In the 1870s, when ranchers and farmers discovered the land was government-owned and, thus open for settlement, they mi-grated to the plains and settled along the Salinas River and Estrella Creek. By 1879, they had planted 3,000 acres to barley and wheat. The results were poor, though, and some gave up. But, there were still 40 families living in the Estrella district in 1880 — enough to support a school and a Protestant church.

The little non-denomational Estrella Adobe Church (19.6) — built in 1879 — is all that remains of this once prosperous com-munity. It was the first Protestant church in northern San Luis Obispo County and served the religious needs of Protestant pioneers until 1912 when various denominations began to build separate facilities. In 1959, the Paso Robles Women's Club began restoring the structure, then in ruins. Today it is a State Historical Landmark. The church itself is not open to the public, but you can view the exterior and wander through the small cemetery that adjoins it. I could spend hours reading the weathered headstones, wondering about the people who lived and worshiped in this isolated land so long ago.

After visiting the church and cemetery, return to Wellsona Road (20.7), turn left and rejoin the main route. The second number in the parentheses represents your total mileage.

113

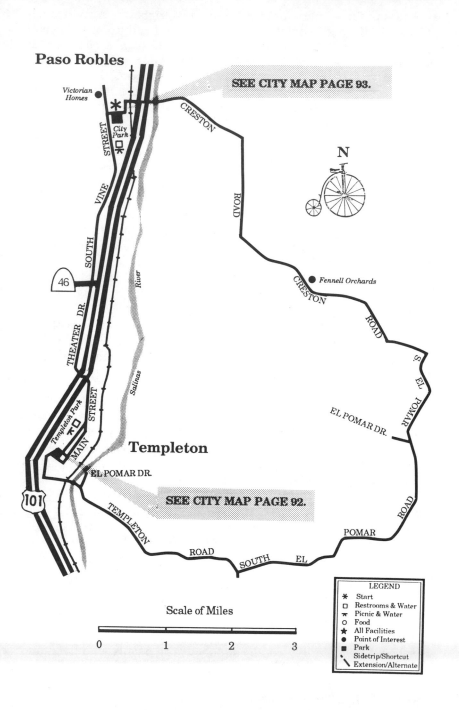

Paso Robles

Victorian Homes

SEE CITY MAP PAGE 93.

CRESTON

STREET

VINE

City Park

ROAD

N

SOUTH

46

River

Fennell Orchards

CRESTON

ROAD

THEATER DR.

S. EL POMAR

Salinas

Templeton Park

MAIN STREET

EL POMAR DR.

Templeton

EL POMAR DR.

SEE CITY MAP PAGE 92.

101

TEMPLETON

ROAD

SOUTH EL

POMAR

ROAD

Scale of Miles

0   1   2   3

LEGEND

✳	Start
☐	Restrooms & Water
⚎	Picnic & Water
○	Food
★	All Facilities
●	Point of Interest
■	Park
↘	Sidetrip/Shortcut
↘	Extension/Alternate

19 — TEMPLETON

RIDE AT A GLANCE

DISTANCE: 23 miles
TRAFFIC: light to moderate
BIKE LANE: yes, on Creston Road and Vine Street
RATING: moderate

Those of us who are used to living in cities or, perhaps, on a few acres in a semi-rural area, find it difficult to comprehend the vast amounts of land granted to Mexican citizens living in California in the early 1800s. The five ranchos located in northern San Luis Obispo County — Huerhuero, Santa Ysabel, Santa Margarita, El Paso de Robles and Asuncíon — occupied a total of 116,412 acres. To me, that's mind boggling.

This ride from Paso Robles to Templeton and back puts the size of the land grants in perspective. With the exception of the few miles spent pedaling in the city of Paso Robles, you stay within the boundaries of the 17,774 acre Rancho Santa Ysabel, granted to Francisco Arce in 1844. And, that's one of the smaller grants. The granddaddy in the North County is the 39,225 acre Rancho Asuncíon, spanning the Salinas River southwest and southeast of Templeton.

Start the ride in Paso Robles City Park (see the Paso Robles map at the beginning of this section). The park has restrooms, water, picnic facilities and charm. And, it has memories. In the early 1930s, the Pittsburgh Pirates held spring training in Paso Robles. Their training field — bounded by 6th and 4th Streets on the north and south and Spring and Pine Streets on the west and east — was just south of the park. After a hard day of practice, players — including Honus Wagner, the Hall of Fame shortstop — headed for the Paso Robles Hot Springs Hotel (now the Paso Robles Inn) for a soak in the soothing mineral waters. More likely than not, they also spent some time relaxing in this park which has been a Paso Robles institution since 1897.

Start your odometer on the corner of 12th and Pine Streets (0.0) and head east on 12th. After crossing the Southern Pacific Railroad tracks, turn left on Riverside Avenue (.1) then right on 13th Street (.2). After you cross the Salinas River (.3), 13th Street becomes Creston Road.

Creston Road is busy at this point, winding through the residential and commercial fringes of town. But, there's an official bike lane here. After the golf course (2.7), the road narrows a bit. When it narrows even more (3.3), you're out of town and rolling through Santa Ysabel country.

115

The Paso Robles area is noted for its vineyards and almond orchards and you pass both on your way to Templeton. But apples also figure into the agricultural picture. It's estimated that at least 400 commercial acres of apples are growing in the North County. If you're cycling through here in late summer or fall, stop in at Fennell Orchards (5.1) — one of about 14 growers in the North San Luis Obispo Apple Growers Association — for tree-ripened apples and freshly pressed cider.

Creston Road continues to roller-coaster through ranches, farms, oak-dotted hills, vineyards and pastures to South El Pomar Road (7.1). Turn right here and follow this narrow, winding road up a gentle grade — tempered by rollies — into the hills. The land out here is unspoiled. You may see cattle, sheep and an occasional farmhouse or barn, but mostly it's wide open country with little or no traffic.

While climbing, you pass El Pomar Drive (8.9). Don't let that confuse you. Continue straight on South El Pomar Road and roll through farmland and almond orchards. The gentle climb peaks at 11.4 miles and then the fun begins. At first the descent is twisting, turning and fast and the view of the Santa Lucias in the distance is fantastic. Then it gentles down a bit (11.7), but you continue to descend to Templeton Road (13.2) where you turn right, climb a short hill, then ride a wonderful set of rollies through pastures dotted with sheep, cattle, horses and oaks to the junction of Templeton Road and El Pomar Drive (16.3). Stay on Templeton Road (that means a left turn!), cross the Salinas River (16.5), turn right on Old County Road (16.8) and follow it to Templeton Park (17.3).

Templeton owes its beginnings to Chauncey Hatch Phillips and the West Coast Land Company. Phillips bought the Santa Ysabel Rancho and portions of the El Paso de Robles and Asuncíon — a total of 63,000 acres — and persuaded the Southern Pacific Railroad to route its tracks through his land to the new town he planned to build. Immediately after the purchase, the 500 square miles of land was surveyed and subdivided into small ranches and town lots. Phillips called his new town Crocker, in honor of the vice president of the railroad. But, there was already a town by that name in California. So, Crocker became Templeton, in honor of Templeton Crocker, the vice president's son.

Within 90 days of its founding, Templeton boasted three hotels, three general stores, a drug store, a meat market, a shoe shop, two blacksmith shops, five saloons, a lumber yard, two barber shops, a post office with daily mail service and about 30 homes. That's pretty amazing when you consider all the wood for the structures came by boat to Cayucos and then was hauled by wagons over York Mountain. By 1887, the Presbyterian congregation in town had built a church. It stands today on the corner of 6th and Crocker Streets, across from the park.

Phillips and the West Coast Land Company donated the land for the park you're resting in. The only string attached was that it was to be — forever and always — a public park. Nobody in Templeton had a problem with that. Today the tree-shaded park — graced by a lacy white gazebo and a caboose — is enjoyed by residents and visitors alike. Playground equipment, a swimming pool, picnic and barbecue facilities, restrooms and water are available. And, on Saturday mornings, there's a farmers' market. All in all, a perfect place for a cycling respite.

When you leave the park, head east on 5th Street. If you'd like to sample local wines, turn right on Main Street (17.5) and pedal one block to Templeton Corner (corner of 6th and Main Streets). This establishment serves as a tasting room for about 15 local wineries that are too small — in size or staff — to operate individual tasting rooms. It's a great way to sample a variety of unique wines that you might not find otherwise. It also has a good deli. If you're not interested in food or tasting, turn left.

Templeton has kept its old west charm, right down to the feed and grain operation that dominates the "skyline". Grain comes to town by rail from the midwest. Once it's ground and mixed, local ranchers use it as supplemental feed for their cattle grazing on the thousands of acres of pastureland surrounding town.

While the Presbyterians built their church of redwood, Templeton's Swedish community chose to build its Bethel Lutheran Church of brick. They made the bricks on the banks of the Salinas River then layed one on top of the other, according to their memories of similar structures in the old country. One of their members hand carved the chancel rail and the pulpit. The church, which stands in Templeton's tree-lined residential section, served the religious needs of Swedes throughout the county. Services in the beautifully simple church were conducted in Swedish until 1935. If you'd like to visit the church, turn left on 3rd Street (17.6). It's just a block off Main, between Crocker Street and Old County Road. If not, continue straight on Main Street.

Templeton's heyday waned when the railroad pushed south to Santa Margarita in 1889. But, the home Chauncey Phillips built for his family remains as a reminder of the days when Phillips advertised his boom town as a "Canaan, overflowing with milk and honey." Phillips sold the house, located at 91 Main Street (17.8), to Hartwig Wessel in 1891 and it remained in the Wessel family for 73 years. Since then, it has had several owners. Today it is the Country House Inn, a bed and breakfast inn.

Like Templeton Feed and Grain, the Templeton Livestock Market (18.3) is a way of life for local ranchers. Every Saturday

117

The Chauncey Hatch Phillips Home, Templeton.

morning, urged on by an auctioneer's call, ranchers gather to buy and sell all types of livestock. A mere nod of the head or raising of the hand is all it takes. It's simple, but effective, and fun to watch.

Once past the sales yard, Main Street sweeps to the left, crosses over the freeway (18.7), then ends at Theater Drive (18.8). Turn right and follow this less-than-glamorous frontage road — which becomes South Vine Street at Highway 46 (20.5) — through a mixture of Victorian and newer homes to 12th Street (23.1). The house on the southwest corner, built in 1890, is one of the town's original residences. If you'd like to see more of these lovely painted ladies, stay on Vine for a short sidetrip through a very pleasant residential section. If not, turn right on 12th Street and return to Paso Robles City Park (23.4).

The hot springs that once beckoned travelers are just a memory today. But, the Paso Robles Inn remains a city landmark. Before you pack it in, take a stroll through the inn's beautiful gardens, complete with flowers, trees, streams and fish ponds. Remember, you're treading where Pittsburgh Pirates once did.

Cemetery, Mission San Miguel Arcángel.

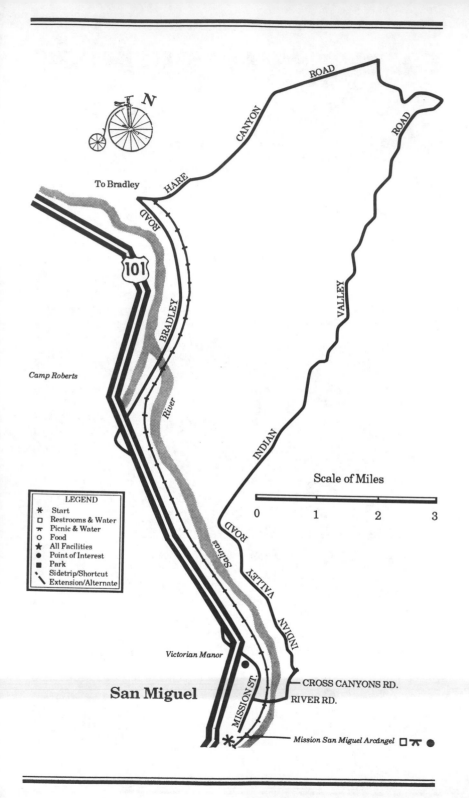

N

To Bradley

101

Camp Roberts

HARE CANYON ROAD

ROAD

ROAD

BRADLEY ROAD

River

VALLEY

INDIAN

Scale of Miles

0   1   2   3

LEGEND
* Start
□ Restrooms & Water
🛫 Picnic & Water
○ Food
★ All Facilities
● Point of Interest
■ Park
⋮ Sidetrip/Shortcut
╲ Extension/Alternate

Salinas

INDIAN VALLEY ROAD

Victorian Manor

●

San Miguel

MISSION ST.

CROSS CANYONS RD.

RIVER RD.

* 🛫

Mission San Miguel Arcángel □ 🛫 ●

20 — INDIAN VALLEY AND HARE CANYON

RIDE AT A GLANCE

DISTANCE:	30 miles
TRAFFIC:	non-existent to moderate (on Highway 101)
BIKE LANE:	wide shoulder on Highway 101
RATING:	moderate to difficult
CAUTION:	no water, food or services

There are rides that lead somewhere specific: a park or a restaurant or an historical monument. There are others that travel through small towns and resorts. Then there are rides that lead nowhere in particular with no scheduled stops along the way. These are the ones we do for the sheer pleasure of cycling. This ride, from San Miguel out Indian Valley and back, is one of those. No glitz, no glamour, no shopping, no museums, no afternoon tea at a Victorian inn. Nope. Just pleasant cycling, pure and simple.

The ride begins at Mission San Miguel Arcángel (see the San Miguel map at the beginning of this section). This mission, founded in 1797, is a working church run by Franciscan friars who, since 1929, have been responsible for the authentic restoration and preservation of the structure. Before or after your ride, be sure to take the self-guided tour through the buildings, garden and cemetery. There are public restrooms near the gift shop and museum, and water and picnic facilities are available.

Start your odometer at the front door of the mission chapel (0.0) and head north on Mission Street through the town of San Miguel. Pedaling through this quiet town, it's difficult to believe that, in 1887, it was a bustling community with 40 licensed businesses thanks, mainly, to the Southern Pacific Railroad. It enjoyed a second boom during World War II when the Army built Camp Roberts on property just north of town. During those years, the community thrived, catering to the needs of the soldiers stationed at the camp. Camp Roberts closed following the war and many of San Miguel's businesses closed with it. Today, the camp is maintained as a training facility, but the number of personnel stationed there is small compared to the wartime complement. And, with transportation readily available, most of the soldiers tend to bypass San Miguel in favor of larger cities. So, San Miguel waits patiently for its next boom.

Turn right on River Road (.6), cross the Salinas River (1.0), turn left on Cross Canyons Road (1.2), then left again on Indian

Valley Road (1.3). Indian Valley Road roller-coasters as you pedal back into the hills. At the Y (2.6), stay left. It's wide open country back here. Some cattle, an occasional farmhouse, a peek now and then at the river. At the top of a rise (4.0), you get a glimpse of Camp Roberts across the freeway to the left. Then, at 4.7 miles you cross into Monterey County and leave all views of the freeway and civilization behind.

As you pedal along the river, the hills begin to close in and soon you're down in a valley, surrounded by gently sloping, oak-dotted hills. Turn left on Hare Canyon Road (13.5), cross the river (13.7) and climb over the hills that separate Indian Valley from Hare Canyon. The climb crests at 15.0 miles and you zip downhill into the canyon via a single lane track that can hardly be called a road.

All of this land is private, much of it government-owned. You often see tank tracks running up and down the hills through the dense oak forests — a reminder that Camp Roberts and civilization are just over the ridge on the right. The road rolls up and down, but the general direction is down. In fact, you're in for a glorious five mile descent.

Turn left on Bradley Road (21.0) and follow the railroad tracks and the river to Highway 101 south (24.0). You have no alternative but to ride on the freeway here. But, it's not a well-traveled section and there is a wide shoulder. As you pedal past Camp Roberts, you re-enter San Luis Obispo County (26.0).

Take the San Miguel exit (27.9) which becomes Mission Street. The Victorian Manor (28.6) is a bed and breakfast inn perched in the middle of a Morgan horse operation. The house, hardly Victorian, was built in the early 1940s by John R. Livingston as the headquarters of his Rancho del Rio Salinas. But, it's a close replica of his turn-of-the-century mansion in Chicago, hence the name.

Follow Mission Street and the railroad tracks past the Purina Chows operation (29.3), through town and back to Mission San Miguel Arcángel (30.3).

Don't forget to tour the mission. The Franciscan fathers have preserved the feeling of history and antiquity here. It's a step back in time — a perfect way to end a pleasant day of cycling.

APPENDIX

CYCLING WITH YOUR CAMERA

by Joseph A. Dickerson

How many times have you cycled down a country road, marveled at the scenery, then cursed yourself for not bringing a camera? You're not alone. Most bikies remember to pack a jacket, the sun screen and the granola bars, but they pedal off without a thought about photographing their adventures.

Whether you consider yourself an amateur or a professional photographer, you can shoot good pictures on your bicycle jaunts with a bit of pre-planning.

EQUIPMENT

When traveling by car, it's easy to throw all of your gear in back and take off. But, when you're traveling by bike, space and weight are major considerations.

I've devised three different outfits that I carry for various trip lengths. You can modify these suggestions to fit your own equipment inventory or method of working.

For day trips, I carry a compact rangefinder camera. The new models with "auto-everything" are great. You can, of course, use a 110 pocket camera, but the 35mm rangefinders give much better results, especially if you like to shoot slides.

I also carry a Star-D pocket tripod. It's sturdy, very convenient and handy for time exposures and self-timer shots. There are other excellent small tripods on the market, but make sure you get a sturdy one. Sometimes I substitute a photographic C-clamp for the pocket tripod — it's sturdy and can clamp your camera to a variety of objects, including your bicycle.

To complete my mini-outfit, I include skylight and polarizing filters, lens shade, cable release, lens cleaner and tissue, film and a medium-size heavy-duty plastic trash bag to stuff all my gear and film into when (notice I didn't say *if*) it rains. Today's electronic cameras don't take kindly to the wet.

For longer trips, or trips where there is likely to be more variety in photographic subjects, I carry a 35mm SLR fitted with a 35-105mm or 28-85mm zoom lens. I find this zoom range takes care of about 90 percent of my shooting and is still compact enough to be easy to carry and retrieve from my bike bag. I also carry the same filters and other essentials mentioned for the mini-outfit, plus a small flash unit. To expand my outfit for extended bike excursions, I add a longer lens — usually a 70-210mm zoom, plus a 24mm wide angle lens and a second camera body.

I have found that the easiest and safest method of carrying cameras and accessories on my bike is to pack it all in the handlebar bag. It's within easy reach and, when I'm off the bike, I can easily take the whole outfit with me. And since the handlebar bag uses a suspension system, it absorbs a lot of the road shock which rack-mounted bags would tend to transmit to the camera gear.

I use a bag that has aluminum inserts in the sides and provides an extra measure of protection. It's not compartmentalized, so I pack the lenses in individual padded pouches. But, there are handlebar bags made specifically for camera equipment. Check with your bicycle dealer for specific brands.

THINGS TO SHOOT

Once your gear is packed and you're on the road, the photographic opportunities are limitless. Take lots of shots that contain local color. Mission San Luis Obispo de Tolosa or the Piedras Blancas lighthouse interspersed with shots of road signs or other things that establish locale really help a slide show communicate what your trip was all about. And, if you're on an extended trip, it's nice to include photos of your bike loaded for the road. If you're riding with a group, have someone get some shots of you on your bike. If you're traveling solo, put your camera on a tripod and use the self-timer. It's a bit tricky, but with practice it can work quite well.

Include some "trick" shots in your bike tour photography, too. One effective technique is to combine a flash exposure and panning at a slow shutter speed. This will give you a sharp, brightly lighted subject against a blurred, slightly darker background. First select a slow shutter speed (you might want to try 1/15 to start with) and make an overall exposure reading. Adjust the aperture to give one stop less light than this reading calls for. For example, if the correct ambient-light exposure is 1/15 at f5.6, set your lens to f8, and your subject will be correctly exposed while the background will be one stop darker.

Along with action shots and local color, be sure to take photos that show the folks in your biking group. Sitting around the campfire enjoying a local wine, pigging out on fresh baked goodies, enjoying an unscheduled dip in the sea, fixing a flat tire while local kids ask a million questions — these are the things that speak of the fun and adventure of cycling. It's all pretty heady stuff. And, as a two-wheeled, free-spirited photographer, you'll record images your steel-and-glass-encased counterparts can only dream of.

Joseph A. Dickerson is an avid cyclist and professional photographer whose travel and cycling photographs have appeared in many national publications. He is a Contributing Editor with Petersen's PhotoGraphic Magazine.

EQUIPMENT

Unless you're really an animal, you will want at least a 10-speed bicycle for most of the rides in this book. However, the rides rated *easy* can be done on three- and five-speed machines.

If your bike is well-maintained, the chances of having to do major repairs on the road are slim. But, you should at least be prepared to patch a tire or adjust a derailleur. Tools can be carried in a handlebar bag, a small pouch that fits under the seat or in a rack pack on the rear rack. And, remember, if you're traveling with a group, not everyone has to carry every item. Just be certain the person with the patch kit isn't a rabbit who will leave you and your flat tire in the dust. The following is a list of suggested tools and equipment to carry:

ESSENTIALS
Change for a telephone call — Pump and patch kit
Tire irons — Two water bottles

HANDY ITEMS
Spare tube — Crescent wrench — Allen wrenches (3, 4, 5, 6mm)
Socket wrenches (8, 9, 10mm) — Compact repair book — Lock
Hand cleaner and rag — Small pair pliers — Chain tool
Spoke wrench — Pocket pro "T" wrench
Standard and Phillips screwdrivers

FOR EXTENDED TRIPS
Spare tire — Spare cables — Spare spokes
Spare nuts and bolts

SAFETY AND CONVENIENCE ITEMS
Bicycle helmet — Sunscreen and lip balm — Rear view mirror
Odometer or bicycle computer — Dog repellent — Jacket
High energy snacks — Camera and film — Binoculars
Tights, leg warmers or sweatpants

Please wear a bicycle helmet. Head injuries are the primary cause of fatalities in bicycling accidents. In California, any child riding as a passenger on a bicycle *must* wear a helmet. It's the law.

CYCLING CLUBS AND TEAMS

CAL POLY WHEELMEN — racing — contact: Jim Delany, c/o Math Department, Cal Poly State University, San Luis Obispo, CA 93407, 805 756-2395.

G.S. SAN LUIS CYCLING TEAM — racing — sponsor: Pro Spoke Cyclery, 971 Higuera Street, San Luis Obispo, CA 93401, 805 541-3600 — contact: Rob Himoto.

NORTH COUNTY CYCLING CLUB — touring, recreation, racing — contact: Wes Hatakeyama, North County Schwinn Shop, 8710 El Camino Real, Atascadero, CA 93422, 805 466-2366.

SAN LUIS CYCLING CLUB — racing — sponsor: Spirit Cycle Works, 399 Foothill Boulevard, San Luis Obispo, CA 93401, 805 541-5673 — contact: Bob Sukoski

SAN LUIS OBISPO BICYCLE CLUB — touring, recreation, racing — contact: Wayne Williams, P.O. Box 1585, San Luis Obispo, CA 93406, 805 543-5181.

ANNUAL CYCLING EVENTS

CUESTA SPIRIT BIATHLON — Cuesta College — October and April — 10K run and 40K bike — individual or team competition — contact: Warren Hansen, 805 544-2943 ext. 289.

GREAT WESTERN BICYCLE RALLY — Mid-State Fairgrounds, Paso Robles — Memorial Day Weekend — clinics, rides, camaraderie. Contact: Laverne Boethling, GWBR, P.O. Box 7000-617, Redondo Beach, CA 90277, 213 540-0521.

LIGHTHOUSE CENTURY — September — 100 or 50 miles — easy pedal up Highway 1 to the Piedras Blancas lighthouse and return to SLO — contact: Wayne Williams, SLOBC, P.O. Box 1585, San Luis Obispo, CA 93406, 805 543-5181.

SAN LUIS OBISPO CRITERIUM — downtown SLO — late May or early June — world class bicycle racing — all categories — top cycling personalities — 20,000 spectators — contact: John Rogers, SLO Recreation Department, 805 549-7305.

WILDFLOWER CENTURY — Creston — April — challenging 100 or 50 miles through the flower-carpeted hills and plains of northeastern SLO County — contact: Wayne Williams, SLOBC, P.O. Box 1585, San Luis Obispo, CA 93406, 805 543-5181.